The Generativity Civilization

Robert R. Carkhuff, Ph.D.

Contributors:

George Banks, Ph.D.
Andrew H. Griffin, Ed.D.
Richard C. Sprinthall, Ph.D.

Published by: HRD Press, Inc.
                   22 Amherst Road
                   Amherst, MA 01002
                   800-822-2801 (U.S. and Canada)
                   413-253-3488
                   413-253-3490 (fax)

ISBN 978-1-61014-373-8

Editorial services by Robert W. Carkhuff
Production services by Jean S. Miller
Cover design by Eileen Klockars
Promotion by Swift Global Media

The Generativity Civilization

Contents

Foreword: America—Rising Above Injustices! vii

Foreword: Can We Shoot Straight? ix
    Andrew H. Griffin, Ed.D.

Chapter 1: "The Tech High Riots" 1

Chapter 2: "The Springfield Debacle" 15
    Introduction and Overview

Chapter 3: "Position, Organize, Process" 21
    Community Generativity

Chapter 4: "Relate, Participate, Generate" 35
    Cultural Generativity

Chapter 5: "Generator, Innovator, Commercializer" 51
    Socioeconomic Generativity

Chapter 6: "The Human Universe" 59
    Generativity Civilization Designs

Chapter 7: "The Civilized Culture" 67
    The Socioeconomic Outcomes

Chapter 8: "The McLean Project" 75
    From Community to Culture to Socioeconomics

Chapter 9: "The Springfield Miracle" 83

Chapter 10: Freedom and Generativity 89

Chapter 11: The Generativity Civilization 105

References 115
    Human Sciences 117
    Information Sciences 121

Carkhuff Body of Work 123

About the Authors

Among the most-cited scientists of the 20th century and already the most prolific in the 21st century, Robert R. Carkhuff, Ph.D., is the author of *The Human Sciences.* His full biography and body of work may be viewed on the following websites:

www.carkhuffgenerativitylibrary.com

www.carkhuff.com

www.mcleanproject.com

About the Contributors

George Banks, Ph.D.
Co-Founder
The McLean Project

Andrew H. Griffin, Ed.D.
Executive Director, Community Development
The McLean Project

Richard C. Sprinthall, Ph.D.
Executive Director, Design and Assessment
The McLean Project

FOREWORD

America—Rising Above Injustices!

No one has synthesized the American mission more clearly than Paul Johnson, author of *A History of the American People* (N.Y.: Harper Collins, 1997):

> First, can a nation rise above the injustices of its origins and, by its moral purpose and performance, atone for them? All nations are born in war, conquest, and crime, usually concealed by the obscurity of a distant past. The United States, from its earliest colonial times, won its title-deeds in the full blaze of recorded history, and the stains on them are there for all to see and censure: the dispossession of an indigenous people, and the securing of self-sufficiency through the sweat and pain of an enslaved race. In the judgmental scales of history, such grievous wrongs must be balanced by the erection of a society dedicated to justice and fairness. Has the United States done this? Has it expiated its organic sins? (p. 3)

From Springfield to Cyberspace

The mission of the Springfield **Community Capital Development (CCD) Project** was simple yet profound:

CCD MISSION

Prosperity with equity!

This CCD mission was fulfilled by the core of effective ingredients of The New Science of Possibilities:

- Relating to Human Potential
- Empowering Human Potential
- Freeing Human Potential

The same principles transfer to projects everywhere in the universe.

While planning to incorporate the underdeveloped peoples of the world in projections of the future IT market, we must also empower all people involved in the different systems of Generative Human Processing:

- Individual Processing Systems
- Interpersonal Processing Systems
- Interdependent Processing Systems

In turn, these human generativity systems empower us to engage and implement the Socioeconomic Processing Systems that we require to generate the productivity and prosperity that our socioeconomic systems require:

- Organizational Processing Systems
- Community Processing Systems
- Cultural Processing Systems
- Economic Processing Systems

Together—Preparatory and Culminating—they constitute the Socioeconomic Systems of Global Growth.

All systems incorporate processing systems. All helpers and builders embrace the systems in order to maximize the building potential of the systems and, in so doing, actualize their own human potential.

We initiated the process of socioeconomic processing in Springfield. We must now transfer the human and Socioeconomic Processing Systems to all peoples aspiring to enter the IT marketplace.

There is no function for the individual if not improved performance. There is no function for the socioeconomic systems if not improved productivity. There is no function for civilization if not improved growth and prosperity.

The Master Plan, as it were, projects incorporating another three billion people in the IT market in the next decade. Mostly from undeveloped or developing cultures and countries, these people are devoid of the skills, knowledge, and attitudes they require to generate the socioeconomic prosperity of great civilizations.

To simply make these people dependent minions of the masters of their destinies means a continuation of the servitude of their work and the slavery of their minds.

To profoundly transform these people by empowering them in the Human Generativity and Socioeconomic Processing Systems makes them masters of their own destinies and collaborators in building a world civilization.

RRC

June 14, 2014
McLean, Virginia

FOREWORD

Can We Shoot Straight?

Andrew H. Griffin, Ed.D.
Executive Director
Community Development
TheMcLeanProject.com

"Can he shoot?"

A very heated argument was being held among the members of the Black American Nascent Group, better known as "BANG." Bob, at that time, was the only white on the floor who was invited by me to join this very prestigious all-black basketball team. I knew Bob could really shoot because of our day-to-day workouts in the American International College gym where we served as co-directors at its Human Relations Center. The issue of having a white person on the team began with a few whispers and finally became loud enough that Bob could hear the challenge. His ability to shoot became more evident to all as he made shot after shot. Yet the disgruntlement became very loud and evident for all to hear. Finally, I challenged them—asking them the question **"Can he shoot?!"** Bob continued to make basket after basket, and the team ended up winning the tournament. As the saying goes, "Case closed!"

Can Robert R. Carkhuff shoot? His accuracy in shooting has sent him way beyond the basketball court (where we went 64–2 over two seasons). His "shooting" has taken him into homes, public and private school systems, higher education, businesses, governments, ghettos, prisons, hospitals, churches (even to Pope John Paul), and countries throughout the world.

The Generativity Civilization outlines the systems needed for human resource development that leads to prosperity, participation, and peace. Let me say that again—*The Generativity Civilization* outlines the systems needed for human capital development that leads to generativity. If you are willing never to be satisfied with yesterday's answers, then read this book. *The Generativity Civilization* calls on the reader to maximize one's full potential in a systematic way so that he/she can pass it on to another, just as Carkhuff outlines in his references of Human Sciences—explore, understand, act, and use your feedback system to grow ad infinitum. Failing to do so means that you become part of the problem instead of part of the solution.

I recently returned to Springfield, Massachusetts, where I had the pleasure of working with Bob, Bernie Berenson, and George Banks, and was heartbroken to see the plight that has developed within my birth city. Springfield—once known as the "City of Homes" and home to the Springfield Armory, Massachusetts Mutual and Monarch Insurance Companies, Smith & Wesson, Webster publication, Springfield College, American International College, Fisk Rubber Tire Company, and Friendly's Ice Cream Company—is now relying on the passage of a state law to become one of the cities to house gambling casino facilities as its way of actualizing its potential.

My brief tour around the city found American International College, Springfield College, and Western New England College, along with the University of Massachusetts growing beautifully or expanding. However, in the City of Homes the "homes" primarily surrounding the colleges have been eliminated, abandoned, and/or in much need of repair. The organizations and programs, such as the Springfield Action Commission, Model Cities, Real People's Congress, New Careers, and Northern Educational Services, designed to provide knowledge and skills for those in need, have been abandoned and forgotten.

What happened to "The Springfield Miracle" that avoided the catastrophe that all other cities and towns experienced in the 60s? What did we learn? What happened to the human relations specialists? What happened after the concerned people left? What is going on with the new generation? Is it too late? What happened to those in charge? Does the absence of the threat of violence mean we are to stop growing? Does the absence of angry people on the news mean we are to stop relating? Does the absence of publicity mean we don't care? Does building iron gates, installing electronic devices, hiring more police, setting higher goals make a difference? From Carkhuff's view, of which I support, the answer is a resounding "NO!" We must challenge ourselves to go in the areas where we have the most difficulty and mine the fields for all of the diamonds found in each of us. Failing to do so means we are quitters and will only work with those whom we believe have the obvious potential.

Carkhuff clearly reminds us that "Quitters never win and winners never quit." He exemplifies the practice "Difficulty is no excuse for surrender." **Can he shoot!!!** Ask anyone who has had the good fortune of knowing and working with him. Ask Bernice, his Proverb 31:10-31 wife who is joined at the hip with him as she multitasks in the raising of six children (6 boys, 3 adopted multi-racial) and two granddaughters (African Americans).

Ask those with whom he teaches and works daily. Just as any winning coach, his demands are high, fully expecting us to use the fundamental tools practiced, using the unique knowledge and skills needed to provide creativity never seen before. He labels our creativity, "generativity."

Yes, Carkhuff once again responds to the question "Can he shoot?" Get the answers from all of those who had the privilege of working with him. Physically demanding, intellectually stimulating, emotionally challenging, socially open, and above all, guided by a spirit that is open for all to participate regardless of who we are.

It is my honor and privilege to work with Bob Carkhuff, a person who has opened his heart, soul, mind, family, friends, and home to all people who are open to give as well as receive, and to never give up regardless of the cost. We who have the privilege of knowing him, his colleagues, and family are truly blessed.

Knowing and working with him requires us to ask ourselves daily: "Do we remain open to learn, to grow, and to share because we know the future is modeled in the exemplary performance of the leaders who are attempting to commit fully to becoming free and prosperous in the 21st century civilization?"

The most powerful social and spiritual experience of my life occurred at "the bottom of the pit." Young white men were riding into "the hill" and firing their shotguns. Young and old, male and female, the blacks ran off the streets and into the doorways. Since the marauders had done this before, the leaders of BANG were agitated and sought to remedy this. I knew an explosion was coming at the cost of many human lives. I was at wit's end when I went to Bob with my dark conclusion. Bob spoke simply:

> Spiro Manolakis is the adult leader of The White Citizen's Movement. Meet with him at NAACP Headquarters. The mission is to prepare your world for the next generation—your grandchildren as well as his.

I did invite Mr. Manolakis. He did come. We did negotiate. We prepared the world for our grandchildren. The crisis was over. No one died!

Now the real issues are ours:

- Can we transform our once-beautiful 'City of Homes' into an empathically-related 'City of Communities'?

- Can we become a generative culture that creates its own answers to our ongoing crises?

- Can we become an entrepreneurial civilization that generates its own prosperity?

Carkhuff has always taught: "The essence of civilization is reciprocity—'The Golden Rule'."

"Can he shoot!!!"

The real issue is ours—and it is spiritual as well as social:

"Can we shoot?"

"Can we shoot straight?"

"This Never Happened!"

Dedication to Captain Dan Shea, **"Guardian Angel"** of the HCD Project

Captain Dan Shea, Springfield Police Department, is legendary for his expressions that probably saved the lives of hundreds of citizens.

Upon approaching a "war scene" where hundreds of police had surrounded more than 60 well-armed militants, Shea processed the situation and announced the following conclusion:

This Never Happened!

The officers returned to their duties. The militants returned to their neighborhoods. No one died. Both groups went on to make incredibly substantive contributions to their families and communities.

Although Captain Shea has expired, he extended his life-long mission, **"To Save and Protect,"** to his enduring spiritual mission:

"We are all children of God!"

This really did happen!

Chapter 1

"The Tech High Riots"

The school crises did not begin at Technical High School on November 5, 1969 when black and white students attacked and hurt one another violently.

The school crises began when each black and white child registered and entered school. Whatever his or her level of adjustment upon entering school, the black child was to learn in very systematic ways that he or she was an inferior element in a white system. The process is subtle, so subtle in effect that its effects are hardly noticeable immediately. One Technical student described the process in this manner:

> It is as if they have asked me to carry an additional feather on my back for each day that I attend school. I now feel that I am carrying a ton of feathers, and I don't know how to get rid of them. But they're not mine!

Even if we accept the validity of the indices of performance, we must reject the sources of these deterioration effects (Carkhuff, 1971):

- Black pupils enter school at levels of achievement not functionally different from white pupils.

- With each year of schooling, while the white students fall increasingly below comparable national norms, the black students fall increasingly below the white students.

- Black students exit school by disproportionately higher dropout rates and significantly lower student achievement rates.

The sources of these determination effects were summarized in The National Advisory Commission's "Report on Civil Disorders (1968)."

The Preconditions of Civil Disorder

The Preconditions of Social Failure

One of the major contributions of the Kerner Commission Report (1968) was to discern and delineate those conditions that constituted the essential ingredients of civil disturbance. Citing the complex and interacting factors, "varying from city to city and from year to year," the Kerner Commission felt, nevertheless, that certain fundamental matters were clear:

- Attitudinal factors
- Political factors
- Economic factors
- Housing and population factors
- Educational factors

Attitudinal Factors

Of these, the most fundamental is the racial attitude and behavior of white Americans toward black Americans.

Race prejudice has shaped our history decisively; it now threatens to affect our future.

- White racism is essentially responsible for the explosive mixture which has been accumulating in our cities since the end of World War II.

- Among the ingredients of this mixture are:

  - *Pervasive discrimination and segregation* in employment, education, and housing, which have resulted in the continuing exclusion of great numbers of Negroes from the benefits of economic progress.

  - *Black in-migration and white exodus,* which have produced the massive and growing concentrations of impoverished Negroes in our major cities, creating a growing crisis of deteriorating facilities and services and unmet human needs.

  - *The black ghettos* where segregation and poverty converge on the young to destroy opportunity and enforce failure. Crime, drug addiction, dependency on welfare, and bitterness and resentment against society in general and white society in particular are the result.

  - *Frustrated hopes* are the residue of the unfulfilled expectations aroused by the great judicial and legislative victories of the Civil Rights Movement and the dramatic struggle for equal rights in the South.

  - *A climate that tends toward approval and encouragement of violence* as a form of protest has been created by white terrorism directed against nonviolent protest; by the open defiance of law and federal authority by state and local officials resisting desegregation and by some protest groups engaging in civil disobedience who turn their backs on nonviolence, go beyond the constitutionally protected rights of petition and free assembly, and resort to violence to attempt to compel alteration of laws and policies with which they disagree.

  - *The frustrations of powerlessness* have led some Negroes to the conviction that there is no effective alternative to violence as a means of achieving redress of grievances, and of "moving the system." These frustrations are reflected in alienation and hostility toward the institutions of law and government and the white society which controls them, and in the reach toward racial consciousness and solidarity reflected in the slogan "Black Power."

> – *A new mood* has sprung up among Negroes, particularly among the young, in which self-esteem and enhanced racial pride are replacing apathy and submission to "the system."
>
> – *The police are not merely a "spark" factor.* To some Negroes, police have come to symbolize white power, white racism, and white repression. And the fact is that many police do reflect and express these white attitudes. The atmosphere of hostility and cynicism is reinforced by a widespread belief among Negroes in the existence of police brutality and in a "double standard" of justice and protection—one for Negroes and one for whites.

These are powerful mixtures. Let us examine their dimensions insofar as they can be ascertained in the Springfield, Massachusetts, community.

In general, the Kerner Commission cites social, political, economic, and educational conditions as constituting "a clear pattern of severe disadvantage for Negroes compared with whites." Specifically, the Commission investigated the factors of all of the various levels of intensity. The recent eruptions in Springfield, Massachusetts, began at the educational level. Before examining the educational factors, let us examine the superstructure within which these factors operate.

Political Factors

One of the first factors pointed to by the Kerner Commission was the political structure including in particular the policing, justice, and grievance functions.

> • The proportion of Negroes in local government was substantially smaller than the Negro proportion of population. Only three of 20 cities studied had more than one Negro legislator; none had ever had a Negro mayor or city manager. In only four cities did Negroes hold other important policymaking positions or serve as heads of municipal departments.

Let us examine Springfield in this regard.

- One of nine city councilors is black, although under the present Plan A Strong Mayor form of government, the black population is denied ward or precinct representation.

- Springfield has never had a black mayor.

- Blacks hold no important policymaking positions other than those federally funded programs calculated to alleviate the existing conditions; i.e., presently the Springfield Action Commission and formerly the Model Cities Program.

- One of over 30 heads of municipal government is black, and his province is specifically Intergroup Relations; i.e., dealing with relations between city government and the black community.

With regard to police and grievance functions, the following national picture emerged in the Kerner findings:

- There have been a number of recent instances of difficulties in police–community relations including the Octagon Lounge incident, the Course Square incident, the Winchester Square incident, and the Lebanese–American Club incident.

- While the responses of older blacks are generally positive to police, the evidence from questionnaires indicates that the attitudes of blacks under 21 years of age are negative toward police, with many believing that they are a stimulus rather than a response to tension.

- While approximately 7 percent of the almost 300-man police force is black, one holds the responsibilities of a high-ranking officer.

- One of six police commissioners is black.

- The human relations commission, the only formal grievance mechanism, is generally regarded as ineffective by the black community and by its past directors and by many of its members.

- There is a generalized attitude among young blacks concerning different tracks of justice represented in recent cases: Whites kill whites and they receive suspended sentences; blacks kill blacks and receive a six-month sentence; blacks kill whites and receive life sentences.

- The differential administration of justice and protection is best illustrated by a contrast of two recent cases involving men with similar backgrounds.

  - In case A, a dozen police officers appeared to testify against a black man accused of assault and battery upon a policeman. However, with the services of a prominent lawyer and letters of recommendation from prominent citizens, the man, while convicted, was assessed a fine of $25.00.

  - In case B, a black man appeared alone, in his own defense, on a breach of peace charge involving refusing to move at the order of a police officer. He was convicted and sentenced to 6 months in the county jail.

Another major area of consideration involves economic dimensions, particularly employment and consumer factors.

Economic Factors

Economic factors laid the basis for much of the frustration in the black community, as seen by the Kerner Commission.

- Negroes were twice as likely to be unemployed and averaged 70 percent of the income earned by whites and were more than twice as likely to be living in poverty.

- Equally important is the undesirable nature of many jobs open to Negroes and other minorities. Negro men are more than three times as likely to be in low-paying, unskilled or service jobs. This concentration of male Negro employment at the lowest end of the occupational scale is the single most important cause of poverty among Negroes.

- The results of a three-city survey of various federal programs—manpower, education, housing, welfare, and community action—indicate that, despite substantial expenditures, the number of persons assisted constituted only a fraction of those in need.

- Ghetto residents believe that they are "exploited" by local merchants, and evidence substantiates some of these beliefs. A study conducted in one city by the Federal Trade Commission showed that distinctly higher prices were charged for goods sold in ghetto stores than in other areas.

Let us examine the Springfield community with regard to economic factors.

- The unemployment rate for blacks of approximately 9 percent is nearly double the overall unemployment rate of approximately 5 percent for the Springfield community.

- Several thousand black and Spanish-speaking families exist upon incomes of $3,000 or less per year.

- The number of blacks in trade unions is so negligible as to be infinitesimal.

- The first black fireman was recently appointed and assigned duty at the Winchester Square firehouse.

- There are so few black-owned small businesses as to make the percentage of the total business population essentially infinitesimal.

- There are no black-owned large businesses.

- The jobs available to blacks continue to be those at the lower end of the continuum.

- Federal programs have serviced only a fraction of those in need.

- Concentrated Employment Program, one of the few potentially positive factors on the employment scene, will shortly have the control of its key components shifted from the community leadership to the Division of Employment Security, which was unable in the past to demonstrate effectiveness in helping the hard-core unemployed and underemployed.

- Concentrated Employment Program, one of the few potentially positive factors on the employment scene, will shortly have the control of its key components shifted from the community leadership to the Division of Employment Security, which was unable in the past to demonstrate effectiveness in helping the hard-core unemployed and underemployed.

- Model Cities thus far has failed in terms of achieving its intended goals in the economic area. The few projects that have succeeded have been a function of the efforts of other, more effective agencies.

- While shopping prices at major food markets are not discriminatory in terms of prices, smaller local merchants charge significantly higher prices. The issue of the quality of products is yet to be investigated.

Another finding of the Kerner Commission concentrated on the problems of housing and population changes, including the related problems of health and recreation.

Housing and Population Factors

Housing and population factors contribute to the overall climate for civil disruption, as viewed by the Kerner Commission.

- Within the cities, Negroes have been excluded from white residential areas through discriminatory practices.

- Just as significant is the withdrawal of white families from, or their refusal to enter, neighborhoods where Negroes are moving or already moved into. About 20 percent of the urban population of the United States changes residence every year. The refusal of whites to move into "changing" areas when vacancies occur means that most vacancies eventually are occupied by Negroes.

- The result, according to a recent study, is that in 1960 the average segregation index for 207 of the largest United States cities was 86.2. In other words, to create an unsegregated population distribution, an average of over 86 percent of all Negroes would have to change their place of residence within the city.

- Between 2 and 2.5 million Negroes—16 to 20 percent of the total Negro population of all central cities—live in squalor and deprivation in ghetto neighborhoods.

- Crime rates, consistently higher than in other areas, create a pronounced sense of insecurity in ghetto populations.

- Poor health and sanitation conditions in the ghetto result in higher mortality rates, a higher incidence of major diseases, and lower availability and utilization of medical services.

- Poor recreation facilities and programs is one of the most significant of the deeply-held grievances.

Let us examine Springfield with regard to housing and population factors.

- Zoning and averaging techniques are employed by municipal authorities to obscure blatant differences in the living conditions of blacks and whites.

- Nearly one-half of the housing units in the Winchester Square neighborhood are rated substandard.

- Of the approximately 4,000 units declared substandard in 1960, more than 50 percent were those housing black families.

- Whites are moving out of central city neighborhoods and blacks are migrating in.

- Blacks have limited opportunities to move into white residential areas.

- Health and sanitation conditions are significantly worse in the black community than in Springfield at large.

- The differential treatment of blacks and whites in health and recreation is best typified by the statistics of two of the community's key centers: the Dunbar Community Center, which serves a population that is approximately 98 percent black, and the Springfield Boy's Club, which now services a population that is approximately 97 percent white (having been moved from an area where it serviced a population that was approximately three-fourths black). The Dunbar Center services a population of approximately 9,000 city residents or approximately 40 percent more than the Boy's Club, which services a population of approximately 6,600. Dunbar services an average of about 380 children a day, or approximately three times the number of children seen at the Boy's Club daily. Boy's Club has a budget of $215,000 per year, or nearly four times the budget of Dunbar's $58,000 yearly. Dunbar's building and facilities are valued at approximately $25,000, including land, or less than one percent of the Boy's Club facilities, excluding land, which were built at the cost of approximately $2,500,000 and include a year-round pool, full-length gym, and the services of many professional staff members, which Dunbar does not have.

Now let us turn to the educational situation, perhaps the most currently obvious scene of disruptive activities in Springfield.

Educational Factors

Education is a key ingredient in the consideration of the development of civil disorders, as seen by the Kerner Commission. In the light of the current difficulties, it deserves the most detailed consideration.

- For the community at large, the schools have discharged their responsibilities well. But for many minorities and particularly for the children of the racial ghetto, the schools have failed to provide the educational experience which could help overcome the effects of discrimination and deprivation.

- The hostility of Negro parents and students toward the school system is generating increasing conflict and causing disruption within many city school districts.

- The most dramatic evidence of the relationship between educational practices and civil disorders lies in the high incidence of riot participation by ghetto youth who had not completed high school.

- Blacks are not represented proportionately at any levels within the educational systems.

- The black record of public education for ghetto children is growing worse. In the critical skills—verbal and reading ability—Negro students fall further behind whites with each year of school completed.

- Many more Negro than white students drop out of school.

- The vast majority of inner-city schools are rigidly segregated.

- Another strong influence on achievement derives from the tendency of school administrators, teachers, parents, and the students themselves to regard ghetto schools as inferior.

- The schools attended by disadvantaged Negro children commonly are staffed by teachers with less experience and lower qualifications than those attended by middle-class whites.

- Many teachers are unprepared for teaching in schools serving disadvantaged children.

- Teachers of the poor rarely live in the community where they work and sometimes have little sympathy for the lifestyles of their students.

- Attitudes of teachers toward their students have very powerful impacts upon educational attainment.

- Despite the overwhelming need, our society spends less money educating ghetto children than children of suburban families.

Let us turn to a consideration, again in some detail, of the conditions of education in Springfield.

- The percentage of black students in the Springfield school system is approximately 22 percent (Puerto Ricans are counted as white).

- The percentage of black teachers is approximately 5 percent (none is Puerto Rican).

- At Technical High School where 256 black students comprise 12 percent of the population, 1 of 106 teachers is black.

- At Commerce High School, where 406 black students comprise 22 percent of the population, 3 of 87 teachers are black.

- At Trade High School, where 261 black students comprise nearly 18 percent of the population, 4 of the 102 teachers are black.

- At Classical High School, where 106 black students comprise over 7 percent of the population, no teachers are black.

- One principal out of 48 is black, and she will retire shortly from her grammar school.

- One assistant principal is black.

- One administrative officer (out of well over 80 administrative positions) is black and his responsibilities include directing the federally financed project for the inner-city child.

- The School–Community Relations expert under Racial Imbalance Law and federal funding is white.

- Blacks have no representation (voting or otherwise) on the School Committee.

- The percentage of blacks of total dropouts is approximately double the rate for the city.

- Five elementary schools range from 60 percent to over 90 percent black.

- Four of the five predominantly black schools have been considered substandard in physical facilities.

- The black students start slightly behind in achievement and grow progressively worse. A sampling of predominantly black schools indicates that by grade 6 the children are already approximately a year behind in arithmetic and reading and even further behind national norms on the Iowa achievement tests.

- Black students comprise progressively larger percentages of auxiliary, or special, classes ranging from nearly one-half at the junior high level to nearly three-fourths at the high school level.

- There is objective evidence to indicate that teachers and administrators and Pupil Personnel Service counselors, those formally charged with the responsibilities for individual guidance and counseling, are not functioning adequately on communication dimensions of understanding and initiative conducive to the constructive development and effective learning of students, black and white.

- The Superintendent of Springfield schools and Massachusetts Education Commissioner have acknowledged publicly that our educational system is not servicing minority groups, that teachers need to be re-educated, and that the black community must have a great deal more to say about the administration of their schools.

Summary and Transition

In the face of the increasing racial tensions in the educational settings and the inability of the persons responsible to act constructively to rectify the sources of these tensions, it was the intention of this report to sample the political, economic, housing and population, and educational conditions in Springfield and compare them to the conditions existing in communities around the country prior to civil disturbances. We have done that and we believe that a reasonable person would conclude that the conditions in Springfield do not differ significantly from those in riot-torn cities around the country.

It was not the intention of this report to make specific recommendations. That has been done elsewhere and many times. It can be done again in terms of developing concrete courses of action to ameliorate the difficulties and free the black community for emergence as a full political economic, social, and educational partner. It is the purpose of this report to recommend that the key responsible parties—the mayor and his staff, the superintendent of schools and his staff, and the directors of other key areas of community functions such as the chief of police—read the original Kerner Commission Report as part of their responsibilities. The 1968 Kerner Report has provided a number of useful guidelines for formulating constructive programs:

- Our recommendations embrace three basic principles:
    - To mount programs on a scale equal to the dimension of the problems
    - To aim these programs for high impact in the immediate future in order to close the gap between promise and performance
    - To undertake new initiatives and experiments that can change the system of failure and frustration that now dominates the ghetto and weakens our society

We cannot, in spite of the pleas of our city leaders, afford "a return to normalcy," for "normalcy" has not, as we have seen, been a happy circumstance for a large percentage of our fellow Springfield citizens. In this context, the Kerner Commission notes the following:

- A study of the aftermath of disorder leads to disturbing conclusions. We find that, despite the institution of some post-riot programs:

  - Little basic change in the conditions underlying the outbreak of disorder has taken place. Actions to ameliorate Negro grievances have been limited and sporadic; with but few exceptions they have not significantly reduced tensions.

  - In several cities, the principal official response has been to train and equip the police with more sophisticated weapons.

  - In several cities, increasing polarization is evident, with continuing breakdown of interracial communication and growth of white segregationist or black separatist groups.

Again, this report was written over 50 years ago. It is difficult to understand why so little has been accomplished in such a long time. The only concept that has been forwarded to account for our inability to act is elaborated on in the Kerner Commission Report:

- What white Americans have never fully understood—but what the Negro can never forget—is that white society is deeply implicated in the ghetto. White institutions created it, white institutions maintain it, and white society condones it.

- The importance of this report is that it makes plain that the white, moderate, responsible American is where the trouble lies.

- The Commission itself reflected the inability of American society, dominantly white, to see and treat its Negro citizens fairly.

- It can only be a beginning because, patently, until the fact of white racism is admitted, it cannot conceivably be expunged; and until it is far more nearly eliminated than this Commission—or any fair man—could find today, how can that great commitment of money and effort here recommended even be approached, much less made?

The choice is ours—here in Springfield as well as around the rest of the nation—whether to believe and pursue the American dream and with the black man's help try to make it viable for him—or dash it on the rocks of prejudice and poverty. The Kerner Commission reaches a similar conclusion:

- This is our basic conclusion: Our nation is moving toward two societies, one black, one white—separate and unequal.

The choice is ours: to release the *full* creative potential of the former repressor as well as the formerly repressed, or to continue in the ways in which we were conditioned—to continue on a collision course with the blacks, for they will no longer accept the ways in which they were conditioned. The Introduction to the Kerner Report is relevant here:

> - The rioters are the personification of the nation's greatest shame, of its deepest failure, of its greatest challenge. They will not go away. They can only be repressed or conceded their humanity, and the choice is not theirs to make. They can only force it upon the rest of us, and what this Report insists upon is that they are already doing it, and intend to keep on.

Finally, the conclusion of the Kerner Commission Report is a meaningful way to conclude the present report:

> - One of the first witnesses to be invited to appear before this Commission was Dr. Kenneth B. Clark, a distinguished and perceptive scholar. Referring to the reports of earlier riot commissions, he said:
>
>   "I read that report...of the 1919 riot in Chicago, and it is as if I were reading the report of the investigating committee on the Harlem riot of '35, the report of the investigating committee on the Harlem riot of '43, the report of the McCone Commission on the Watts riot.
>
>   "I must again in candor say to you members of this Commission—it is a kind of Alice in Wonderland—with the same moving picture reshown over and over again, the same analysis, the same recommendations, and the same inaction."
>
> - These words come to our minds as we conclude this report.
>
> - We have provided an honest beginning. We have learned much. But we have uncovered no startling truths, no unique insights, no simple solutions. The destruction and the bitterness of racial disorder, the harsh polemics of black revolt and white repression have been seen and heard before in this country.
>
> - It is time now to end the destruction and the violence, not only in the streets of the ghetto but in the lives of people.

This might have been written in hundreds of communities, large and small, around the country—before and after 1969 and today.

"The Tech High Hopes"

Let us review these findings. The black pupil in Springfield, Massachusetts, enters school with a slightly lower developmental IQ, although he is not functionally different from his white counterpart, with the slight difference due perhaps to the disadvantages of poverty. With time and "education", the black pupil falls further and further behind. He achieves less in critical academic skills than white students. He tends to drop out of school more than white students. The greatest part of special sections for slow learners are drawn from the ranks of black students.

Thus far, we have dealt primarily with the intellectual scars upon the black child. The emotional scars, and now the physical scars, are just as great. Emotionally, we have scarred the black student by conditioning him to experience himself as inferior to the white on critical task performances. Now we have scarred the black student physically by bringing him to form mobs for purposes of physical violence and by making him the victim of other mobs formed for purposes of physical violence.

In addition, we might add emphatically, in designing and implementing a system that provides advantages for the white student, we have scarred him. We have scarred the white student intellectually in that we have not asked him for optimum performance and actualization of his intellect. We have scarred the white student emotionally by conditioning him to experience himself as superior to persons of different races and colors. And now, we have scarred the white student physically by causing him to form mobs for the purpose of physical violence and by making him the victim of other mobs formed for purposes of physical violence.

By the time he gets to high school, then, the black student, already two or more years behind on the average, is seized with a sense of frustration and powerlessness. He feels the weight of the "feathers" that he has accumulated. He knows fully now that the educational family is not his family. At the outbreak of violence at Technical High School, while black students constituted 15 percent of the overall total of high school students, only 8 of the 363 teachers or 2 percent were black, and several of these acknowledged little or no disposition to or communication with the black students. The black student has few, if any, constructive black models available to him.

Indeed, he has never been a member of the educational family. As with any family, the child who is told that he is a member but is not treated as such rebels. He rebels against things that have held him back—often things that he himself does not fully understand—but he rebels. He strikes out at the family that has lied to him. He strikes out at its parents. He strikes out at its members.

When he strikes out he finds out just how much of an outsider he is to this educational family. The teacher-parents are threatened by the unrest. True to form, they are hostile, fearful, anxious, and view the black students' demands as a defiance of authority. They respond with suspension and tightened discipline to avoid the exposure of the fact that there never was any love for these members of this family. Predictably, they blame outside agitators, overcrowdedness, the need for more money, and now drugs. They advocate security guards, the employment of which serves only to heighten school tensions and increases the polarizations already in effect. *These adults "shape up" the children, black and white, to violence in order to avoid the exposure of their own incompetence.* Battle lines are drawn and more conflict ensues. The effects of the battle serve only to reinforce the frustration of the black students. Force is employed primarily against them. Arrests are made primarily from their ranks. Hatred becomes a fire smoldering beneath the surface, exploding periodically in greater and greater intensity.

We can only assume that the adults responsible for the conduct of the city and its educational system are aware of these outcomes. They cannot placate the students by simply assigning as counselors at the high school level five black teachers who were neither systematically selected nor trained for effectiveness. They cannot ease racial tensions by simply creating a third lunch session, for that is clearly treating symptoms rather than sources. They cannot eliminate frustration by increasing it with increased discipline and law and order platforms. They must know this and, accordingly, accept the full responsibilities for the consequences of their efforts.

The real hope lies in the response to the crisis of Technical High School. After surrounding the buildings with hundreds of police officers and trying every known remedy of command-and-control behaviors, the education department finally called in the Human Resource Development or HRD Center. Their advice: Send in the Human Relations Specialists—a trial program empowering people from the streets with crisis management skills! They did so. Maurita Bledsoe and Ronald Carrol moved in the next day using tested crisis management skills:

- The HR specialists divided the school down into black and white groups.
- One HR specialist worked with the black group while the other worked with the white group.
- After five days, the HR specialists brought the groups together to relate.
- The black and white groups related.
- The educators and police officers went back to their assignments.

The rest—as they say—is history! Two Human Relations Specialists had replaced hundreds of teachers and police. The story of "The Tech High Hopes" is the story of "The Springfield Miracle," which follows.

Chapter 2

"The Springfield Debacle": Introduction and Overview

George Banks and I looked out at our trainees, two groups of women—one black, one white. They had been identified by black community leaders as one of the primary "sources of dissension—an insoluble community crisis."

The black women were identified as "Earth Mothers" and the white women were labeled "Suburban Volunteers." The "Earth Mothers" violently rejected the seemingly "righteous efforts" of the suburban women to help out on community crises.

This was our test: if we could enable these groups to learn to relate and work constructively with each other, then the black community would allow us into Springfield.

The test was offered by Andy Griffin, a community leader. Banks and I were confident that we could resolve the crisis by empowering both groups to relate effectively. Our confidence was based upon the research that we had conducted on "Race and Social Class in Helping." Basically, these demographic conditions did not make a difference when the helpers were functioning at high levels of facilitative skills, such as responding and initiating. Empathic responsiveness and operational initiative accounted for success in helping.

It was the summer of 1967, and Springfield, Massachusetts, was in crisis. It met all of "The Preconditions of Civil Disorder" as defined by the Kerner Commission as essential to civil disturbance.

Primary among the preconditions was "The Cycle of Social Failure." Discriminatory practices in all areas taught blacks that they were inferior: their powerlessness to change this practice reinforced the effects of the original teaching. Springfield was on the brink of an explosion of violence (see Figure 1 on the following page).

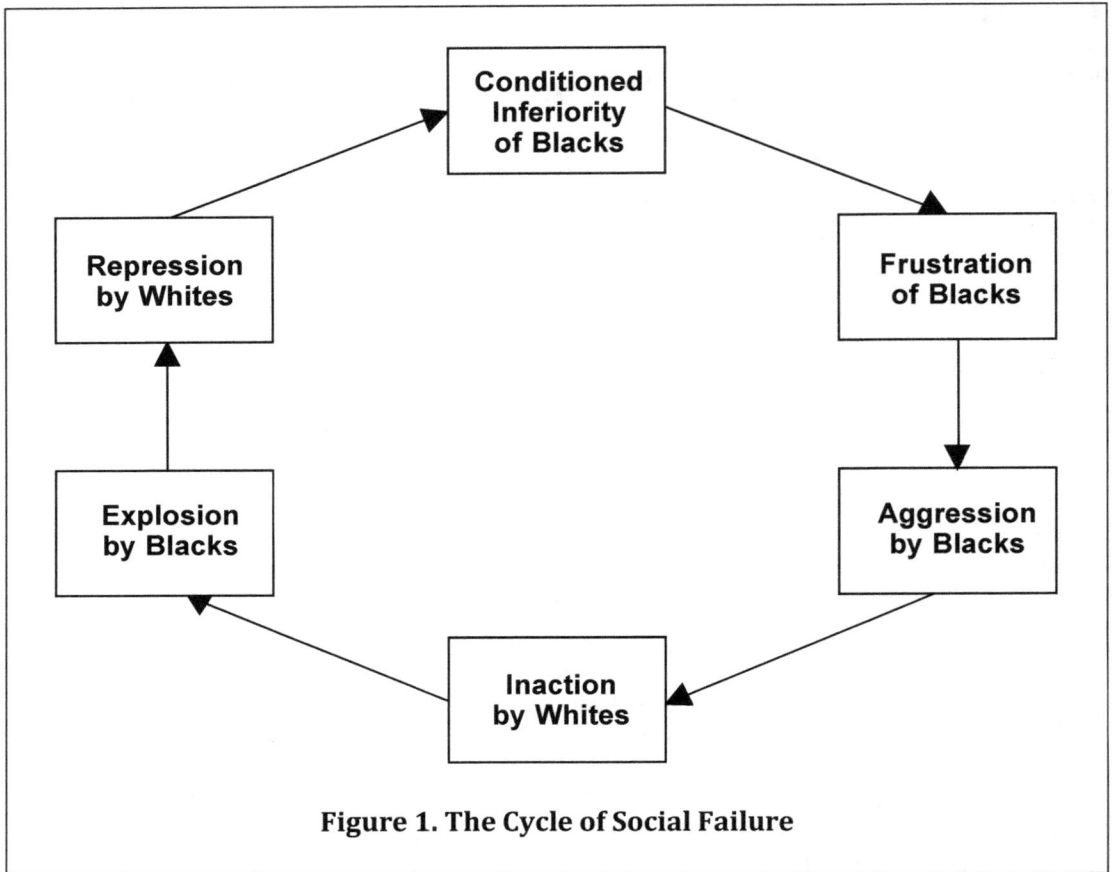

Figure 1. The Cycle of Social Failure

Our design for resolving the "relating crisis" was simple. We labeled it "The Relating Project," and set up the conditions for "reciprocal relating" or "giving and taking" as follows:

- The black women would be trained by Banks, who was black (Weeks 1–2).

- The white women would be trained simultaneously by Carkhuff, who was white (Weeks 1–2).

- The two groups of women would be brought together to relate only after they each had met the criteria of relating effectiveness (Weeks 3–4).

The training design was based upon the findings of our research. We assumed that these women must first learn to relate inside the group before they could relate outside.

In our terms, the women must learn to "relate" before they could "reciprocate." They could only "give" after they had "taken." They could only "take" after they had "given."

At the conclusion of training, the individuals involved—40 in all—met or surpassed all measurable criteria on relating effectiveness.

We had empowered all of the women in relating skills—responding and initiating. When the community evaluators returned after four weeks, they were amazed by the level of relating and working within and between the groups. Some of the group members responded to the evaluators:

"You're overwhelmed by the progress we have made."

"We're empowered by the skills we've learned."

"There's hope for you!"

"The Win–Win Paradigm"

Dick Sprinthall was the initiator of The Community Project and therefore had a much larger perspective than The Relating Project. Indeed, he barely tolerated our test as the entry learning experience to his mission—Saving Springfield. In his words, "It is already one hour to midnight."

In this regard, Sprinthall had several unique perspectives on the crises:

- As Professor of Psychology at American International College, he understood the "island" around which the underclass black and brown communities had congregated.

- As mentor of Andy Griffin, a graduate of the college and the recognized leader of the black community, he understood their sense of hopelessness.

- As consultant to the CEOs of the two biggest corporations in town, Jim Martin of Mass Mutual Life Insurance and Ben Jones of Monarch Life Insurance, he understood corporate fear of being surrounded by the underclass minority communities.

Sprinthall's design was simple: bring in the most powerful human and community resource developers, Carkhuff and Berenson, and unite them with the most powerful black community organizer, Griffin. The results that he foresaw would fit the "Win–Win Paradigm:"

- The members of the black community would "win" by elevating their educational and vocational qualifications and acquiring jobs and earnings.

- The corporations would "win" by making peace with the underclass communities that surrounded them.

- The college would "win" with the reflected benefits, including financial support that would attend their contributions to the resolution of community crises.

All of these "wins" would come to pass with the resolution of community crises. But it was not to be without other crises that upped the ante for the participants involved!

"The Grow–Grow Paradigm"

What Sprinthall had not fully recognized was the precarious nature of the crises:

- A community rebellion of the underclass was coalescing, led by young black militants who were prepared to die in the streets.

- An investor rebellion was silently occurring, which called for the corporations to move their elaborate enterprises into the suburbs away from Springfield.

The net effect of civil disturbances would be to lose both the diminishing sources of wealth for the community and the disappearing sources of hope for the people. As industries fled to more cost-beneficial climes, the people who would suffer most were the disenfranchised underclass populations with increasingly higher rates of unemployment, welfare, criminality, and other indices of dysfunctionality. There were already proposals for "ghettoizing" the underclass communities with "walls and cops." The police already had the rebel leaders "in the crosshairs." Springfield was indeed in a precarious condition.

It was already ten minutes to midnight!

In other words, the conditions for both the corporations and the people who surrounded them were deteriorating and exacerbating. Consequently, the requirements for success were elevated. "The Grow–Grow Paradigm" was born.

"The Grow–Grow Paradigm" began with an understanding of the fruitlessness of "Win–Win" when neither of the parties had anything to offer. "Grow–Grow" was generated as follows:

All parties must grow before either party can relate.

Like the women in conflict, all parties must elevate before any parties can relate.

Accordingly, we defined our strategic objectives as follows:

1. To empower the corporations to grow

2. To empower the community to grow

3. To relate each to the other

Concerning the corporate objectives, we invited them to participate in Community Development Seminars in our graduate program where we explored and initiated projects for all aspects of community development. We empowered the corporations to make tangible internal and measurable community innovations. Perhaps most dramatic at this time, we introduced their corporate leaders to the use of computers in their actuarial-based insurance industries. In so doing, we contributed dramatically to the future growth of their industries.

Concerning the community objectives, we empowered waves of candidates with educational credentials and job skills for both the private and the public sectors. In this context, the program graduates lobbied the local corporations for entry-level positions with the promise that their future performances would be "interchangeable" with those of the current corporate employees. This proved to be the case. We contributed dramatically to the future growth of the community.

Most important, we brought representatives together periodically in "Real People's Congresses," where all parties involved shared their problems and co-processed to generate solutions. Together, we designed and developed the next sources of industrial and community development:

- Information technology-driven

- Human technology-supported

To be sure, "The Springfield Miracle" was born and transported across the state to Boston and other communities, which, supported by the IT development in and around Route 128, soon evolved into "The Massachusetts Miracle."

Perhaps most important of all was the birth and growth of "The Generative Processing Systems," which were dedicated to thinking "outside the box." These systems generate solutions to human problems that are not currently available.

Chapter 3

"Position, Organize, Process":
Community Generativity

The most problematic of all areas of human endeavor is that of developing human potential. Many of us have been conditioned to believe in the inherent superiority and inferiority of different populations. Indeed, it is our own conditioning that has led us to believe that the underclass is genetically determined.

Generativity is born in the community along with the infants of all sorts of homes and families. No child is excluded from the potential for generativity by their birth-families, schools, communities, cultures, or nations. The critical issue here is this: what do the families, schools, communities, cultures, and nations do to stimulate, facilitate, and actualize the potentially unlimited brainpower with which each child is born?

Figure 2 illustrates the Basic Community through which an individual takes a journey:

- **Homes and neighborhoods** prepare the infants with linear conditioning and mechanical responses.

- **Schools and training** empower the children with discriminative learning skills and introduction to information responses.

- **Colleges and technology centers** empower the students in generative individual processing with an introduction to human processing systems.

- **Government and service agencies** empower the citizens in generative organizational processing with an introduction to organizational processing systems.

- **Business and industry** empower their employees in generative marketplace processing with an introduction to marketplace and environmental processing systems.

As may be noted, each of the community components may be related to the other components. This is the key to effectiveness in "The Generative Community."

Thus begins the individual's journey to maturity: generativity in communities, in cultures, in nation-building, and civilization. This paradigm will serve as a foundation to guide you in building your images of civilization. They are processable! Their architecture is actionable! They are generative!

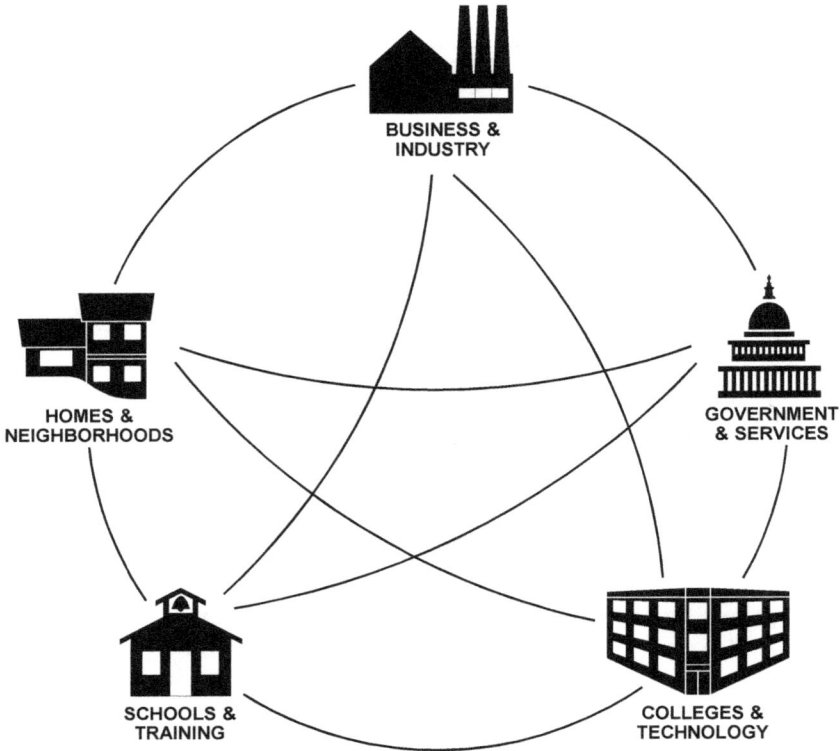

Figure 2. The Generative Community

Generative Homes

History is replete with studies of the effects of neglect upon child development. Scientists, psychologists, and nutritionists have all concluded that neglect is a powerful "depressor variable." When neglect intervenes in a child's life, the effects are disastrous: physically, emotionally, and intellectually. Clearly, the environment in the form of parents and their surrogates did not stimulate and support these children.

Their parents did not know how to do so because no one had ever taught them how to do so. They could not teach their children because no one had ever taught them. They could not support their children's learning because no one had ever supported their own learning.

The neglected children, many of them superior in intellectual resources, were destined to live with minds and bodies enslaved by intellectual limitations just as surely as the children's ancestors had been enslaved by chains. Many of these children were to subsist below poverty levels on their poor farms. Some were to move to the city and join the ranks of the unemployed, or they were to become less than full persons because of financial dependence on the welfare system. Others were to opt for a criminal career ladder and end up in prison or the morgue.

All because we did not help them to actualize their superior potential.

And no amount of guidance will serve to guide them down the path to education, no amount of rehabilitation counseling will help them to actualize their potential, no amount of psychotherapy will help them to emerge as full human beings, no amount of correctional counseling will give them back their freedom.

Because we are not ready for our own fulfillment, our own actualization, our own emergence, our own freedom, we will not give these children theirs.

The Facilitative Effects of Stimulation

Some people rise above their bonds to study the effects of a human environment upon little human beings. This brings us to the studies of children in Milwaukee by Rick Heber and associates. In the 1970s, they studied the relationship between poverty and mental functioning. It divided the children of intellectually-challenged welfare mothers into two groups. In the experimental group, the researchers carefully selected teachers and trained them to work with the infants of the mothers on welfare. The teachers, in turn, trained the mothers of infants to respond sensitively to the children, and to stimulate and reinforce their learning activities.

In other words, all parties involved worked together to maximize the impact of the environment at the point where the child was going through the greatest growth. And they did this through skills training. Skills for the teachers, skills for the parents, skills for the children.

What do you suppose the difference in I.Q. was between the experimental and control infants in the welfare study after three-and-one-half years?

10 points? 20 points? 30 points?

The differences between the children who were nourished intellectually and those who were not was 33 points.

Think of it! The study focused upon children who, in the absence of continuous responsiveness and stimulation, are destined to live out their lives as city slum dwellers at best—and at worst, may have no lives at all!

The children in the welfare study, in the presence of continuous responsiveness and stimulation, may exercise their superior abilities to rise above their places of origin.

The difference?

The enslaved group was abandoned to the "benign neglect" of the playpen and the TV set.

The free group was saved by committed and disciplined people who put the human being back into the learning equation.

But most of all, the free group was saved by skilled people who taught skills to people who, in turn, taught skills to other people.

In the instance of neglect, the unattended children may drop by more than 30 I.Q. points over a period of several years. In the instance of facilitation, the attended children may gain more than 30 points over a period of several years.

The difference between facilitation and neglect is the difference between life and death itself. And it is the use—or the absence—of skills that makes all the difference!

Generative Schools

All educators are familiar with the "Achievement Deficit." With each year of schooling, the black children fall further and further behind on the "Achievement Curve."

Well, some black parents worried long and hard about it. And they were determined to do something. There were black leaders who taught them that if black people get involved, their kids will learn fast. Back in the 1990s, the people of Chester formed the first charter school in Pennsylvania: The Chester Village Charter School.

They formed a black school board. They appointed a black headmaster. They increased the ranks of black teachers to teach their 100% black students. And they fell further behind on the "Achievement Curve"!

Falling Further Behind

Not only did they fall behind in achievement but also in attendance, deportment, and all other indices of functionality. Daily, when arguments broke out at the lower class levels, the upper class students emptied their classes and brawled in the halls. Teachers, themselves, were not safe from assaults and flying missiles like erasers and chalk. Many of us know the scene because we saw it on *The Wire.*

Outside the school, the reputation was as a "feeder school" to the violent public high school. The "Boyle Street Gang," graduates of the Charter School, served as "Murder, Inc." for the City of Chester: just leave $100 in the right place and you could have anyone assassinated!

To be sure, 85% of the boys over 16 years of age were in the criminal justice system. Nearly two-thirds of the girls over 16 were pregnant and on welfare. Things were out of control!

The leader and the teachers were in a state of depression because the kids were not learning the way they should. They felt that they had done everything that they could do naturally. And they cared! Above all else, they cared! Yet things got "worser" as they say.

Most of all, the kids were in a state of agitated depression. They came in innocent and hopeful. They opened to an experience that they found harmful. They left streetwise and fearful.

Some dropped out. Others "fell out." Most just "passed out"—physically, emotionally, and intellectually. Those who "passed on" found that the Village Charter School had been a training ground for the Chester Upland Public High School: it prepared the students for the retarding experiences which lay ahead.

Getting Ahead

501 out of 501! The Charter School got its rankings in the State of Pennsylvania. It was dead last in achievement. Things could not get any worse. It had become the highest priority for closing in the state—"The failed Charter School."

Now the school faced the feared standards of "No Child Left Behind," the controversial federal legislation. The school's goal was to make "AYP," or "Adequate Yearly Progress," which none of the schools in the district had made before.

Yet the leaders never gave up! They internalized their own inadequacies. They had no finances for consulting and training, so they could not even find prescriptions for the limitations that they diagnosed. Nevertheless, they sought help.

The help came in the form of "The Possibilities Schools" that introduced a new curriculum—literally, "The New 3Rs."

"The New 3Rs" were dedicated to teaching the learners to think. In terms of the conventional curriculum of "The Old 3Rs," the learners were taught to co-process the content with the teachers by employing "The New 3Rs":

- **Relating** to exchange images
- **Representing** images in operational forms
- **Reasoning** with the new images

Both kids and teachers responded with enthusiasm; all had found a new and "awesome" way of learning. They responded accordingly with awesome effort.

The most important thing that "The Possibilities Schools" program did was to install one of those Headmasters who never gave up believing in the kids. His name was John Linder and he was, himself, a "homeboy" from Chester who never gave up hope. He was empowered in "The New 3Rs" and he took an incredible journey into teaching effectiveness. "The Possibilities Schools" now had the model they needed for everyone—teachers and students alike—to emulate.

The second most important thing that "The Possibilities Schools" program did was to install Dale Kelly as the Assistant Headmaster. Ms. Kelly acted as a "lead-teacher" who managed the entire school as if it were her class. She loved every child as her own and empowered every teacher as agents of the children. Indeed, "The Possibilities Schools" now had the agent that they needed to learn from.

Empowered with both model and agent for "The New 3Rs," the students of The Village Charter School went on to break all records for performance. To be sure, it became the only school in the district to accomplish the coveted AYP—above 10% overall.

From 501 to AYP! Here is the rap the students put together and recited:

25

"The Relating Rap"
by the Students of Chester Village Charter School

I.   Village Charter is The Relating School.
     It teaches us The Relating Rule—
     Relate to people and relate to knowledge,
     Relate to skills that get us into college.

II. Above all else, we relate to read.
     To decode our reading, we break down the deed.
     Our guiding rule is "Basic Interrogatives."
     That breaks down into "Viable Prerogatives."

III. "Who is doing what to whom?"
     That's the basic question we have to assume.
     "How and why are they doing their thing?"
     "Where and when?" answers everything.

IV. We relate the same in order to write,
     Who, what, when, where, how and why?
     "5WH" is our formula.
     It makes performers out of us all.

V.   When we began we were the worst,
     Now we know we are the first!
     "We're Number One," that's just deserve,
     We're getting ready to jump the curve.

VI. Village Charter is The Relating School.
     It teaches us The Relating Rule.
     We relate to people and relate to knowledge.
     We relate to skills that get us into college.

Generative Colleges

Of all "The Preconditions of Civil Disorder" defined by the Kerner Commission as the essential ingredients for civil disturbance, the most fundamental is the racial attitude and behavior of white Americans toward black Americans. Racial prejudice has shaped our history decisively; it now threatens to affect our future. The key to unlocking the doors of community crises is empowerment in generative processing.

Civil Disorder

Among "The Preconditions of Civil Disorder", the following are most critical:

- Pervasive discrimination and segregation in employment, education, and housing, resulting in continuing exclusion of great numbers of blacks from "The American Experience"

- Social, political, and economic conditions of inner-city communities constituting a "clear pattern of severe disadvantage for blacks compared with whites"

Indeed, the frustrations of powerlessness had led some blacks to the conviction that there was no effective alternative to violence as a means of achieving redress of grievances and of "moving the system." These frustrations were reflected in alienation and hostility toward the institutions of law and government as well as the private sector of the white society that controlled them. To be sure, it is the great fear of "home-grown terrorists" that will drive the intelligent majority community to once-again invite the minority community to participate in The American Experience.

At American International College, leaders of both the black and white communities were recruited to be empowered in processing interdependently the ongoing crises of their time. In other words, the empowered participants processed in "real-time" to generate solutions.

The American Experience

Clearly, the solution to exclusion is inclusion: full participation in the mission of The American Experience:

- Cultural relating
- Participative governance
- Free enterprise

These became the goals of the first Center for Human Resource Development (HRD). The programs were based upon the "Core of Generativity":

- **Relating** to images
- **Representing** images
- **Reasoning** with images

We began with the human relations skills that enable us to relate not only between groups but within our own groups. Over a month-long program, we divided blacks and whites into groups. Within each group, we empowered the members to relate effectively to each other with interpersonal communication skills. Next, we brought the groups together to relate between groups. The cultural relating was immediately successful and the participants were ecstatic. Cultural relating is the cornerstone of all human endeavor. It led us directly to our next steps.

Since the majority community addressed the minority community with "benign neglect," our "Real People's Congress" committed immediately to defining and implementing a "Shadow Government." Our community leader, Andrew Griffin, became our "Mayor Pro Tem." His mission was to engage all members of the community with one basic question:

"What would you like to do with the rest of your life?"

They answered universally:

"We would like to be everywhere that impacts us."

An incredibly profound answer! We had our assignments. We were off-and-running to meet the needs of our citizens. Participative governance is the core ingredient of The American Experience. It led us directly to our next steps.

Basically, the responses of thousands of citizens directed us to initiate entrepreneurially in both the public and private sectors. We developed our programs in the terms that the people conceived—"from womb-to-tomb!"

- Pre-parenting skills
- Early childhood preparation
- Primary and secondary education
- Private and public sector employment
- Participation in governance
- Participation in politics
- Participation in integrated housing
- Participation in recreation and fitness
- Participation in counseling and guidance
- Participation in bereavement and other benefits

Obviously, in order to accomplish these objectives, we had to define and implement, but we also had to implement new areas of lobbying and publicizing!

The most powerful outcomes were professional:

- In terms of cultural relating, all graduates attended college, and more than 50% were graduated (this from a population with an average 7th grade education).

- In terms of participative governance, all graduates participated in city government, with many assuming leadership roles (Ray Jordan became a Massachusetts State Senator and chaired the Ways and Means Committee).

- In terms of free enterprise, the graduates out-earned the majority community (three of the graduates became millionaires).

Perhaps the most dramatic outcomes were personal as well as beneficial to the community:

- None of the men ever committed another crime (all had criminal records before the HRD program).

- None of the women ever went on welfare again (all had been on welfare before the HRD program).

The formula was straightforward:

Engage the disenfranchised in The American Experience and they will respond as all other Americans have:

- Relating for peace
- Enlightening for participation
- Enterprising for prosperity

The HRD graduates will never stop growing! Generativity is a spiral that never ends!

Generative Government

Back in the late 1960s, the HRD Center in Springfield developed a graduate program in Human Resource Development—Community Resource Development (HRD–CRD). More informally, this program was known as "The Shadow Community," installed because of the "benign neglect" that the majority community and its governance reflected upon their marginal black and brown citizens.

The Shadow Community

The mission of "The Shadow Community" was to bring together representatives of all organizations affecting and affected by HRD and CRD. Accordingly, the center recruited heavily from leaders of the private sector as well as leaders from the public sector and the community-at-large. In their regular sessions, they processed interdependently the critical issues of their time: social, economic, employment, educational, and other areas. For each problem area, the CRD group generated solutions that they then acted upon.

For example, to improve deteriorating socioeconomic conditions in the inner-city, the CRD group contributed to the architecture of "Bay State West," a revitalization of business development in the core of the inner-city.

To improve employment and economics, the CRD group lobbied both the private and public sectors for entry-level positions for which the HRD program was responsible for training and supporting.

Educationally, the CRD group initiated Educational Achievement Programs for those left behind by conventional public education; e.g., New Careers Programs for the old career drop-outs!

Along these lines, "The Concentrated Employment Program" was converted to a college-degree preparation program in which "90-day wonders" received training in core living and learning skills, and specific working skills of their individual choices.

Programs in many other areas such as housing and welfare and criminal justice all followed with astounding results. A 20-year follow-up indicated the following enduring highlights of performance:

- All graduates were gainfully employed, many at executive, management, and supervisory levels, including one who ultimately sat on the Board of Directors of a Fortune 500 firm.

- All graduates went on to complete at least one year of college at many different post-secondary institutions, including one graduate with a doctorate from Harvard.

Moreover, the college in which the graduate program was housed received due recognition. While all colleges in New England experienced significant declines in applications for admissions in the late 1960s and early 1970s, during the years the HRD Center was in operation, American International College (AIC) experienced an increase of 15% to 20% in applications. According to J. Walter Reardon, Vice President, Massachusetts Mutual, and a graduate student in the program, "This was a million-dollar public relations miracle. It was as if parents and their children were saying, 'At least AIC is dealing with the relevant problems of our time'."

The demonstrations were important: marginalized people really can participate and perform in The American Experience.

The implications are profound: what is the majority doing preventing the minority peoples from participating in The American Experience?

Perhaps the most important demonstration of the CRD group was the introduction to computerized contributions to be performed. In these group meetings, Dr. Bernard G. Berenson, a pathfinder in computer applications, introduced the groups to the use of computers. Based as the major industries were upon actuarial data, the computerization came to spur the revitalization of the Springfield insurance industry.

In summary, the major facets of The American Experience were processed in the CRD group in the HRD Center:

- Cultural relating in relations within, between, and among the private, public, and community sectors;

- Participative governance in responding and then initiating proactively to the crises within, between, and among the private, public, and community sectors;

- Entrepreneurial enterprise in generating, risk-taking, and managing new initiatives leading to new enterprises within, between, and among the private, public, and community sectors.

The participants in the CRD group had indeed designed and implemented The Shadow Community. In so doing, they, themselves, were transformed from prime Human Capital to "enlightened citizens."

Generative Business

After all is said and done, it is not the energy crisis that has put America on the edge of bankruptcy—economic, social, and moral. It is the "generativity crisis"!

This crisis in generative thinking spreads virus-like, just below the surface, blurring our abilities to observe and diagnose. Osmotically seeping through our permeable membranes, this virus penetrates the very thought processes of our brains.

The virus brought with it a continuous and incremental reinforcement schedule of benefits—of "quick hit" innovations and successes. Most seductive, it brought with it incalculable wealth—multi-trillion dollar markets that capitalistic society had never known before.

In return, the virus asked that those who participated in its "shell game" forgo any generative thinking. "Outside the box!" became an expression defining the forbidden territories of generative thoughts.

In embracing greed over work, consumption over productivity, the American people abandoned the most powerful thinking in the history of the world:

- The generativity in "Interdependent Cultural Relating," which brought us all phenomena modified by the adjective "human"—human development, human potential, human relations, human resources, human capital, human sciences, human technology, human processing.

- The generativity in "Enlightened Participative Governance," which brought us all phenomena modified by the adjective "enlightened"—enlightened learners, enlightened scholars, enlightened citizens, enlightened representatives, enlightened laws, enlightened justice, enlightened executives, enlightened balance-of-powers.

- The generativity in "Entrepreneurial Free Enterprise," which brought us all phenomena modified by the adjective "entrepreneurial"—entrepreneurial capitalism, entrepreneurial generators, entrepreneurial innovators, entrepreneurial commercializers, entrepreneurial public sector, entrepreneurial private sector, entrepreneurial curricula, entrepreneurial students.

By abandoning our history of generativity, we also abandoned our future in generativity. In so doing, we have lost not only our potentially infinite brainpower but also our potentially eternal souls.

The Generativity Explosion

At the same time in the late 1950s and early 1960s that Jack Kilby was inventing the microprocessor, we were studying human processing. Here are the conclusions of a report we made at the time.

In interviews, we found that what made Kilby's contributions profound were not the products and services he generated, but the generative processes he employed. In other words, Kilby had a thinking system—a processing system—for generating breakthroughs.

31

- **Relating to images**—Immersing in the phenomena for weeks or even months, positioning to elicit the images that they yield to him.

- **Representing images**—Conquering the operations involved and developing preliminary models, systems, and technologies to represent them.

- **Reasoning by exploring**—Exploring the representations by expanding the new possibilistic models, systems, and technologies.

- **Reasoning by understanding**—Understanding new images by narrowing to preferred probabilistic models, systems, and technologies.

- **Reasoning by acting**—Initiating action programs by planning to achieve objectives within the preferred models, systems, and technologies.

Moreover, once he had developed productive images, Kilby shared them with his colleagues. He stimulated them to generate and share their images. Together, they treated all images as input to interpersonal processing of new and more powerful images.

Finally, and most important, Kilby lived and processed interdependently inside the phenomenal images he and his colleagues generated. He dedicated himself along with other phenomenal components to accomplishing the phenomenal functions. He employed the phenomenal processes to enable the components to accomplish the functions. In effect, he merged with the phenomena. What he had generated, he now innovated.

Kilby is the model of the generative innovator. He built models of the phenomenal operations. He processed these operations generatively — individually, interpersonally, and finally, interdependently.

Processing is all about phenomena. Phenomena are the people, data, and things that we encounter in our daily existence. Phenomena may be as small as a skill step in a simple task we must perform or they may be as large as the great missions of our business, our economy, or our society. Every experience is phenomenal.

Phenomena are defined by their operations: the functions they discharge; the components they invest; the processes in which they engage; the conditions from which they derive; the standards they set. In essence, phenomena, themselves, are processing systems: component inputs are transformed into function outputs by generative processes under specifiable conditions and with measurable standards.

Generative processing, then, is about generating phenomena: qualitatively improved images of phenomenal functions, components, processes, conditions, and standards. Ultimately, we learn to live and process within the phenomena we have generated. Generative processing is dedicated to generating qualitatively better and more powerful images of the phenomena with which we work! In short, generative processing is a "best processes" approach to breakthrough thinking. It is what we taught to staff members of the major insurance corporations in the 1960s and 1970s.

Perhaps the most powerful principles that we conveyed to the leaders of the insurance industry in Springfield were those of "entrepreneurial generativity." This was the real genius of the American capitalistic system. From our earliest days, we have been driven by the generativity engines of Franklin, Hamilton, and Washington. Entrepreneurial leaders such as Edison, Ford, and Rockefeller defined the core infrastructure of the 20th century—electricity, combustion engines, motor cars, highways, energy, and finances. Tom Watson, Sr., generated the model for "The Golden Age of American Business" in the second half of the 20th century with systems and sales of business machines and computers.

This was a tradition carried on by J. Walter Reardon. For his graduate thesis, Reardon designed the architecture for transforming the Department of Public Relations at Mass Mutual into the Division of Corporate–Community Communications. This became the platform for "mutual growth" of both the private sector and the community.

The Generativity Solution

As has been demonstrated, every stage of human generativity builds developmentally and cumulatively. This means that each stage builds upon the previous stage. From the perspective of science, each lower-order stage is a precondition for a higher-order stage.

Thus, homes and neighborhoods provide the foundation for schools and training. Similarly, the colleges and technologies build developmentally upon the schools; government and services upon colleges; and business and industry upon government (see Figure 3).

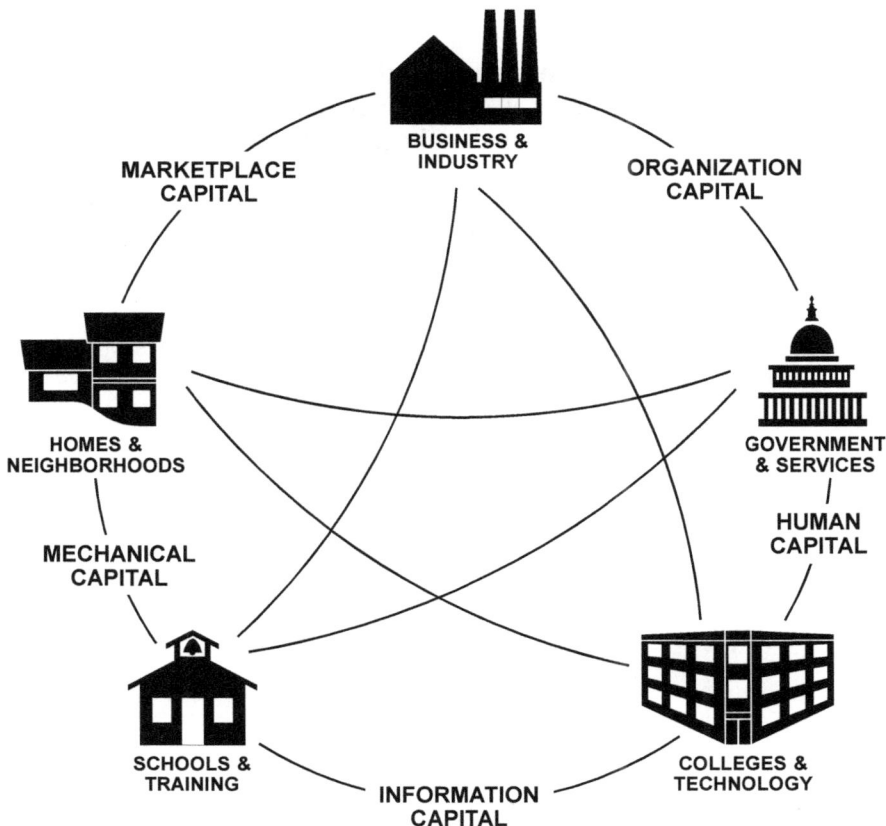

Figure 3. Community Capital

These potent sources of growth operate synergistically to generate the truly capital community, a prepotent source of "The Generativity Solution."

Empowered by the Community Resource Development Programs of the 1960s and 1970s, the results were identified as "The Springfield Miracle"! The historic "City of Homes" had been transformed from the dying industrial town of the 1960s to the thriving Information Technology Center of the 1980s:

> Today, the city's industrial plants have been shutting down, but service industries and small-scale "job shops" have taken their place. The biggest growth has been in the financial services, accounting firms, and insurance companies. All of these factors have converged to reduce unemployment below 3 percent.[*]

In our graduate and undergraduate programs at American International College, the dying industrial town had discovered that it was mismatched to meet the conditions of the evolving Information Age.

Through generative leadership, its community components were aligned to facilitate the instantaneous communication of growth-relevant information. All community components were integrated in "Community Generativity." For example, the minority groups actually reached the standards of performance of the majority groups on indices such as earning power.

This was a glorious time for Springfield and its citizens! Empowered by the "Skyhooks of Generativity," the people had pulled themselves up by their own "bootstraps of growth"—personal, educational, governmental, and business in "The Synergy of Corporate–Community Growth" modeled in the graduate program by Reardon's architecture.

Springfield had risen—like Phoenix out of the ashes—to define itself as a thriving "Information Center." It had reinvented itself as a Generative Community. It had generated its own "Generativity Solution."

---

[*] Nocera, J. The Springfield Miracle. *Newsweek,* June 6, 1988, pp. 45–48.

Chapter 4

"Relate, Participate, Generate": Cultural Generativity

Cultural Generativity is built upon the foundation of Community Generativity. As may be noted, Community Capital Development (CCD) is developmentally and cumulatively the function of the components of Community Generativity.

Just as we experienced "culture shock" nationally, so do communities experience culture shock locally. For example, while Springfield achieved the mission of Community Generativity in the 1970s and 1980s, it was to suffer the shock of losing its generativity in the 2000s.

Empowered by the Community Resource Development Programs of the 1960s and 1970s, community results were identified as "The Springfield Miracle": the historic "City of Homes" had been transformed from the dying industrial town of the 1960s to the thriving Information Technology Center of the 1980s.[*]

"The Springfield Debacle" is yet another story of the transformation, one generation later, to a dying Technology Center at the beginning of the 21st century. It is a story of "Losing Springfield":

> Springfield, the third-largest city in Massachusetts, certainly seems down in the dumps, the victim of a decimated industrial base, middle-class flight and seemingly intractable poverty, all greatly aggravated by years of government mismanagement and corruption that have left it at risk of bankruptcy.[**]

So how did this culture shock happen?

- First, the dying industrial town discovered that it was "mismatched" to meet the conditions of the evolving Information Age. It "reinvented" itself as a thriving "Information Center."

- Second, 20 years later, the dying Information Center discovered that it was "mismatched" to meet the elevated Human and Organizational Requirements of the 21st century. It could not reinvent itself because of a lack of leadership and perspective.

"Cultural Generativity" is no more nor less than an enduring network of communities held together by their commitment to their values of "The Freedom Functions": Cultural Relating, Participative Governance, Free Enterprise (see Figure 4). Indeed, the composite of the integrated efforts of the communities is defined as "Cultural Capital Development" or "CCD'."

---

[*] Nocera, J. The Springfield Miracle. *Newsweek,* June 6, 1988. pp. 45–48.

[**] Belluck, P. City of Homes and Hoops Faces a Long Road Back. *New York Times,* March 12, 2006. p. 12.

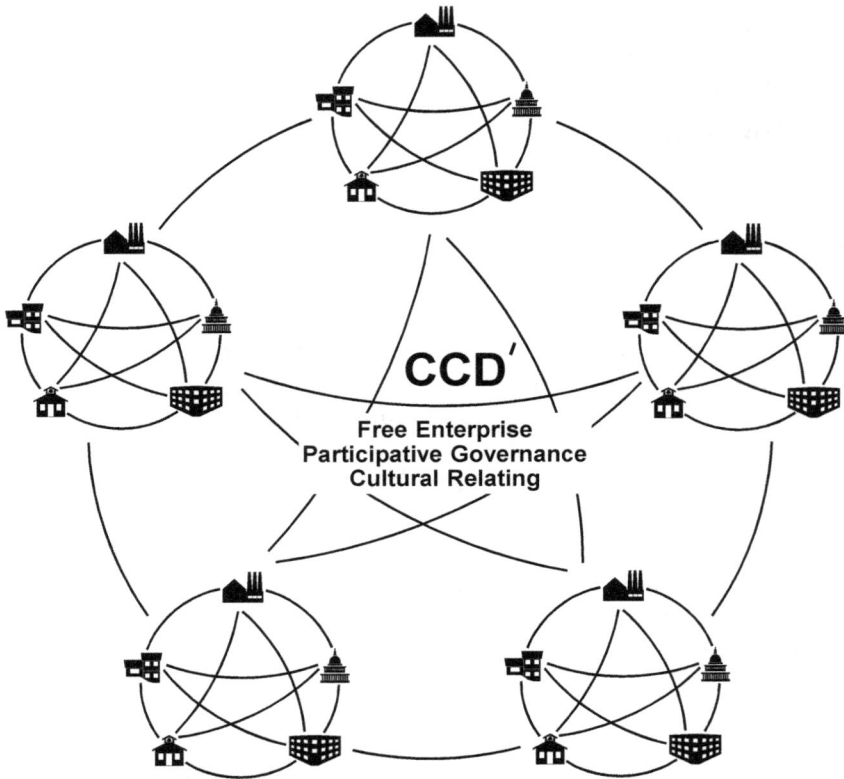

Figure 4. Cultural Generativity

The culture is, to be sure, as generative as the individual communities which, in turn, are as generative as individual and organizational generativity that comprise them. A weak community weakens the culture in which it is networked.

During the initial growth period, the community components were aligned to facilitate the instantaneous communication of growth-relevant information. All community components were integrated in Cultural Generativity. For example, the minority groups actually reached and often exceeded the performances of the majority groups on indices such as work productivity and earning power.

During the later deterioration period, the community components were misaligned with community functions. For example, not only did the minority groups fall dramatically behind on all indices but also the growing underclass was the stimulus to both middle class flight and widespread governmental corruption.

Cultural Degenerativity

The most powerful problem in Springfield's degenerativity was the absence of its community leader, Dr. Andrew H. Griffin. When he left, Springfield lost its cultural integration. No longer did the cultures relate collaboratively. No longer was governance conducted transparently. No longer did the community and the private sector work in harmony in the free enterprise system.

When Dr. Griffin left Springfield for his career in education, Springfield was holding together with high levels of Cultural Generativity. Griffin, himself, was not only the symbol but the model for integration of the cultural functions: cultural relating, participative governance, and economic enterprise (see Figure 5):

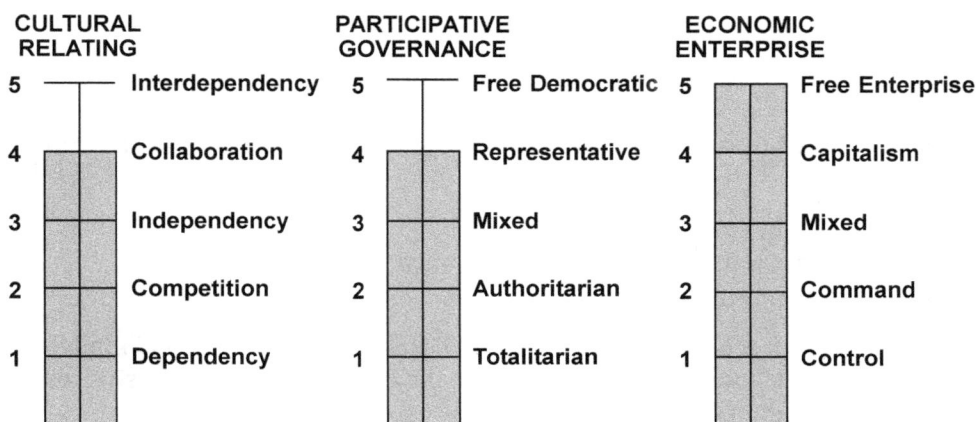

CULTURAL RELATING		PARTICIPATIVE GOVERNANCE		ECONOMIC ENTERPRISE	
5	Interdependency	5	Free Democratic	5	Free Enterprise
4	Collaboration	4	Representative	4	Capitalism
3	Independency	3	Mixed	3	Mixed
2	Competition	2	Authoritarian	2	Command
1	Dependency	1	Totalitarian	1	Control

Figure 5. Springfield Levels of Cultural Functions (1980)

As may be noted, in 1980, Springfield was functioning at high levels for all cultural functions:

- **Collaboration** in cultural relating
- **Representation** in participative governance
- **Entrepreneurism** in economic enterprise

It is noteworthy how Griffin implemented the cultural functions. For him, the cultural functions were incorporated in the Christianity that he espoused. Acknowledging that America was founded upon Judaic-Christian values of relating, participating, and enterprising, it was a natural extension of his religion to model and support the highest levels of collaborating, representing, and capitalizing.

Later, after Griffin's absence for over 20 years, Springfield deteriorated on all of the cultural functions (see Figure 6):

CULTURAL RELATING		PARTICIPATIVE GOVERNANCE		ECONOMIC ENTERPRISE	
5	Interdependency	5	Free Democratic	5	Entrepreneurial Enterprise
4	Collaboration	4	Representative	4	Capitalism
3	Independency	3	Mixed	3	Mixed
2	Competition	2	Authoritarian	2	Command
1	Dependency	1	Totalitarian	1	Control

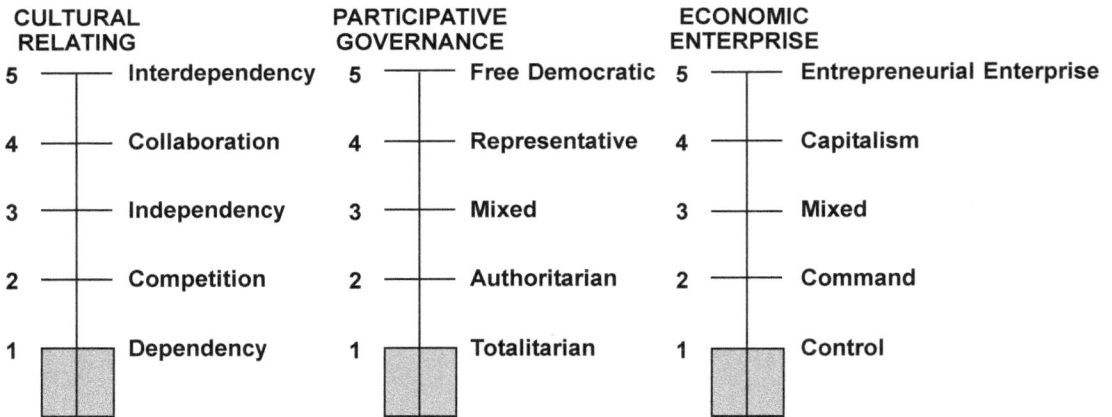

Figure 6. Springfield Levels of Cultural Functions (2008)

As may be noted, Springfield was functioning at the lowest levels of cultural functions:

- **Dependency** in cultural relating
- **Totalitarianism** in participative governance
- **Control** in economic enterprise

In Griffin's absence, no one stepped up to fill the space where he had modeled and integrated the cultural functions. Consequently, the community lost cohesiveness and lost developmental benefits on all indices of new capital development.

Cultural Capital Development

In defining the operations of Cultural Generativity, we have factored the values centering on Cultural Capital Development: cultural relating, participative governance, free enterprise. Together, these values define The Freedom Functions. They emphasize the levels of freedom that cultures must achieve in order to meet the requirements for participation, contribution, and leadership in the Global Village and its marketplace (see Table 1).

Table 1. The Cultural Generativity Architecture

THE CULTURE FUNCTIONS

STAGES OF CCD	Cultural Relating	Participative Governance	Economic Enterprise	
GROWTH ↑				
5. Leader	Interdependent	Enlightened	Entrepreneurial	21st Century
4. Contributor	Collaborative	Representative	Capitalistic	Late 20th Century
3. Participant	Independent	Mixed	Mixed	Mid 20th Century
2. Observer	Competitive	Authoritarian	Command	Early 20th Century
1. Detractor	Dependent	Totalitarian	Control	Pre-20th Century
SURVIVAL				

As may be noted, The Culture Functions define the dimensions of Cultural Freedom for Nations:

- **Cultural relating** or the degrees of relatedness within, between, and among cultures;

- **Participative governance** or the degrees of participation in governance within, between, and among cultures;

- **Free enterprise** or the degrees of freedom in economic enterprise within, between, and among cultures.

Together, The Cultural Functions define The Cultural Architecture for entry and elevation in The 21st Century Global Marketplace.

In 2004, we studied the relationship between Prosperity and The Freedom Functions: Cultural Relating, Economic Enterprise, Participative Government. In Figure 7, we present the relationship of our Freedom Scores and Prosperity measured in Per Capita Gross Domestic Product or GDP.

As may be noted, in the "Power Curve" there is a high relationship between Freedom and Per Capita GDP: high scores on The Freedom Functions earn high GDP and vice versa. This means that, as the Freedom Index moves toward "Free," the Per Capita GDP moves upward many thousands of dollars. Conversely, as the nations move toward "Detractor," the Per Capita Indices move toward low earnings, ultimately numbered in hundreds of dollars per year.

The correlation between Freedom Scores and Prosperity Indices is high. Depending upon the measures, approximately three-quarters of the variability in Prosperity Indices is accounted for by the variance of Freedom Scores.

That correlation is not a perfect one-to-one correspondence due to other factors; for example, some nations that are totalitarian may be also rich in resources such as energy—so they get "middling earnings."

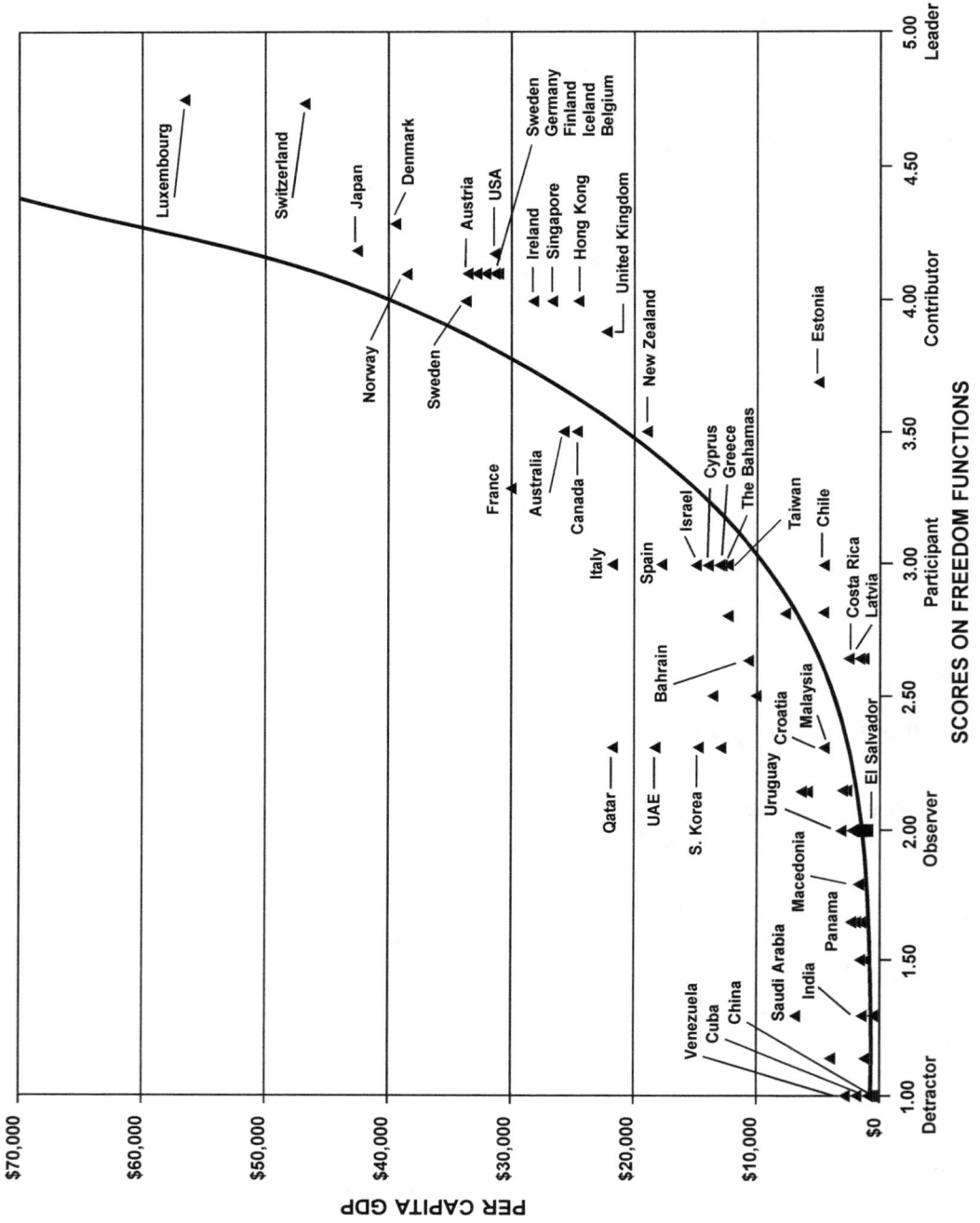

Figure 7. Freedom and Prosperity (Freedom Wars, 2004)

In this context, the figure presents the images of "The Past, The Present, and The Future of Civilization":

- The "Past" is found in the clustered low scores on The Freedom Functions of "The Detractors" who live in a version of "The Pre-20th Century Civilization:"
  - Dependent cultural relating
  - Controlling economic enterprise
  - Totalitarian governance

- The "Transition from The Past to The Present" is discovered in the Middling scores of "The Observers" who live in a version of "The Early 20th Century Civilization":
  - Competitive cultural relating
  - Command economics
  - Authoritarian governance

- The "Present" is represented in the mixed scores of "The Participants" who have only begun to embrace freedom in a version of "The Mid-20th Century Civilization":
  - Independent cultural relating
  - Mixed enterprise economics
  - Mixed governance

- The "Transition to The Future" is found in the high scores of "The Contributors" who are committed to becoming free and prosperous in a version of "The Late 20th Century Civilization":
  - Collaborative cultural relating
  - Capitalistic enterprise economics
  - Representative democratic governance

- The "Future" is modeled in the exemplary performance of "The Leaders" who are attempting to commit fully to becoming Free and Prosperous in "The 21st Century Civilization:"
  - Interdependent Cultural Relating,
  - Entrepreneurial Economics,
  - Enlightened Governance.

Indeed, all peoples of all nations may become free and prosperous. The Freedom Architecture is modeled by The Exemplary Performers on The Freedom Functions. This is the foundation for all Possibilities Civilization.

To be sure, there are no prosperous Totalitarian Nations!

Only nations striving toward freedom receive the Rewards of Freedom.

The Threshold for Prosperity appears to be at The Participant Level of the Freedom Functions (Level 3.0):

- Peoples and nations that relate with Cultural Independence, meaning collaborative or competitive according to the conditions and their requirements

41

- Peoples and nations that engage in Mixed Enterprise Economics, meaning capitalistic or by command as appropriate to their conditions

- Peoples and nations that engage in Mixed Governance, meaning representative or authoritarian according to their circumstances

At the Participant Level, then, nations ranged in the $10,000–$20,000 per capita GDP.

Above the Participant Level, nations and peoples take off in growing and, then, spiraling levels of prosperity. At the Contributor Level (above Level 4.0), the modal earnings were in the range of $30,000 per capita GDP. Approaching the Leader Level (above Level 4.5), a nation such as Switzerland earned above $45,000 while Luxembourg reached over $56,000 per capita GDP.

Below the Participant Level, nations are poor. At The Observer Level (above Level 2.0), where nations had not committed themselves to freedom, the per capita GDP ranged below $5,000. At the Detractor Level where many of the nations are reactive and even destructive, the earnings ranged in the hundreds of dollars.

This, indeed, may be one of the most important correlational figure of our time—or any time! Freedom is directly and powerfully related to generating prosperity and all of its related values—peace and participation!

In summary, we reap what we sow! Put another way, we get what we process for. If we process for freedom in Interdependent Cultural Relating, Enlightened Participative Governance, and Entrepreneurial Economic Enterprise, we will achieve untold possibilities of prosperity and enlightenment.

If, on the other hand, we plan for control in Totalitarian Governance and Command Economics, we will achieve the under-reported problems of isolation, poverty, and ignorance.

In transition, freedom assumes the Infinite Potential of Human Brainpower and empowers us to generate, not only a continuously-expanding economy but also Our Continuously-Changing Destiny. Its adherents learn more and more about more and more until they know a great deal about an Evolving-Everything.

Totalitarianism assumes the finite nature of all resources from which derives an Economy of Scarcity, a Psychology of Stasis, and a Pathology of Discrimination. Its practitioners know less and less about less and less until, finally, they know nothing about anything.

The American Culture Shock

On Flag Day, June 14, 2004, I addressed the first "Freedom-Building Conference" in McLean, Virginia. I remember it well because Flag Day is my birthday. At that time I expressed my disappointing projections of the Bush administration's functioning on the empirically-validated "Three Factors of the Freedom Experience":

- On Cultural Relating, I projected a disastrous decline from Collaborative Relating to Dependent Reactivity.

- On Participative Governance, I projected a precipitous plunge from Democratic Participation to Totalitarian Socialism.

- On Free Enterprise Economics, I projected a desperate fall from Entrepreneurial Capitalism to a Command-and-Control Economy.

To my dismay, all of this has to come to pass.

Perhaps the greatest culture shock in the last 100 years of America was experienced by its citizens in the presidential term of George W. Bush. From an administration that began with the mission of "Compassionate Conservatism," this administration devolved to one that emphasized "Passionate Despotism."

Bush's "Compassionate Conservatism" was to be found in the following "Pre-9/11" goals reflecting his principles:

- Improving the lot of the underprivileged
- Improving our international relations
- Reducing government, taxes, and bureaucracy
- Transforming our national defense structure
- Engaging in bipartisanship, which had characterized his governorship in Texas

Bush was to abandon all of these goals.

"Post-9/11" changed everything. Bush had become "The Wartime President."

- His flagship legislation, "No Child Left Behind" proved a sham in practice.

- His humility in international relations succumbed to the totalitarianism of the neo-conservatives.

- His libertarian intentions were deformed by profligacy in spending, which resulted in larger government and massive debt and deficit.

- His commitment to security was undermined by a "hard-wired bureaucracy" that could not manage the extraordinary defense budgets it received.

- His bipartisan intentions were destroyed by Machiavellian manipulations that produced governance bitterly divided by partisan politics and petty prejudices.

Bush failed on all of his goals.

We, the American citizens, suffered the consequences. When we analyze the characteristics of The American Experience that made us peaceful, participative, and prosperous, we conclude the following about Bush's administration:

- He undermined the uniquely-American Entrepreneurial Capitalism that made us prosperous by conducting a Totalitarian Socialistic Government in the service of the Multinational Corporations that he believed he required in his capacity as "Wartime President."

- He eliminated the uniquely American balance of powers that enabled a Participative Democracy by ruling by edict and intimidation, assuming the powers of Congress, and politicizing the decisions of the Supreme Court.

- Perhaps most disastrously, he transformed our uniquely American "melting pot of cultural relations" back again into a "boiling cauldron" by pouring salt on the wounds of ancient prejudices and hatreds with "divide and conquer" strategies.

Yes, we American citizens know firsthand what culture shock is all about!

Freedom Functions Ratings

U.S.A. 2000—The Producer Culture

Over the last century, then, the U.S.A. defined the emerging requirements of The Global Marketplace:

- Free Cultural Relating
- Free Participative Governance
- Free Enterprise Economics

These are the requirements for entry into the 21st century marketplace. They also define the American Mission. Historically, this is how the U.S.A. was rated by subject-matter experts in 2000.

Cultural Relating

Simply stated, a nation must relate culturally—within, between, and among cultures—in order to join The Global Marketplace. American leaders have always set their goals high on Cultural Relating (see Figure 8). Even transitionally, when they retreated to independency or competitiveness, they never surrendered the ideas of collaborative relating. While their definitions of interdependency may have been limited, they were nevertheless striving toward it.

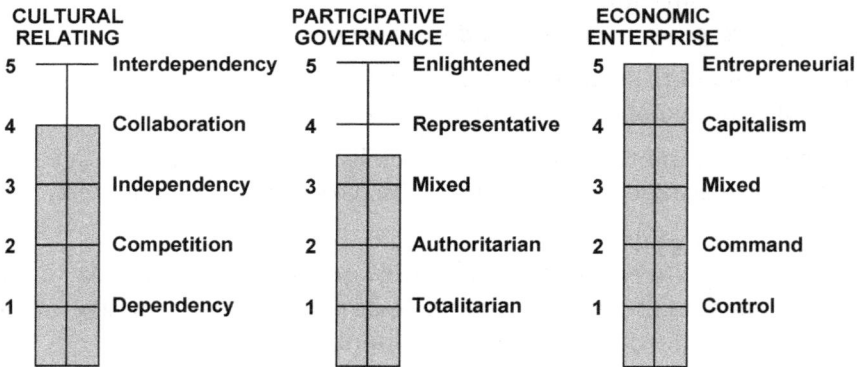

CULTURAL RELATING		PARTICIPATIVE GOVERNANCE		ECONOMIC ENTERPRISE	
5	Interdependency	5	Enlightened	5	Entrepreneurial
4	Collaboration	4	Representative	4	Capitalism
3	Independency	3	Mixed	3	Mixed
2	Competition	2	Authoritarian	2	Command
1	Dependency	1	Totalitarian	1	Control

Figure 8. U.S.A. Levels of The Freedom Functions (2000)

In 2000, the U.S.A. was rated at level 4.0 on Cultural Relating, reflecting its commitment to collaboration without real motivation for interdependency (perhaps as a function of the conflict of individualism with consensus), except within rare homogeneous cultural groupings.

Mixed Governance

The U.S.A. has also been dedicated to Participative Governance at high levels. While its citizens are guaranteed pre-potent policymaking functions by the U.S.A. Constitution, its representative democracy often migrates into a "role reversal" where citizens serve politicians and bureaucrats. Nowhere has American promotion of democracy been more problematic than in attempts to impose it upon foreign cultures. Participating begins with relating to other's frames of reference before empowering them to achieve their own enlightened purposes. That is the true nature of democracy. There is no enlightenment without empowerment! There is no empowerment without relating!

In 2000, the U.S.A. was rated at level 3.5 on Participative Governance (see again Figure 8), reflecting the inconsistent nature of its attempts at making representative governance work; stumbling that led precipitously to representative self-aggrandizement; stumbling that yields disastrously to authoritarianism by default.

Entrepreneurial Enterprise

The U.S.A. has been dedicated to Economic Enterprise at the highest levels. Succinctly, the U.S.A. Constitution, protecting private property and, in an amended form, civil and economic liberties, provides a strong foundation for the nation's free and dynamic economy. In addition, the U.S.A. has taken the leadership in promoting free trade, not only with neighbors in the Western Hemisphere but with nations around the world. While not yet having realized its mission of Universal Free Enterprise, the U.S.A. has been the world leader, par excellence.

In 2000, the U.S.A. was rated at level 5.0 on Economic Enterprise, reflecting its aspirations for entrepreneurial enterprises and reciprocal trade at the highest levels (see again Figure 8). "The Producer Culture" continued on its path in spite of the influence of "The Consumer-Driven Culture." Whatever the obstacles, there would be no vision of The Global Marketplace without America's highly entrepreneurial leadership; there would be no standards for prosperity and, thus, for the evolution of world civilization!

To sum, in 2000, the U.S.A. received relatively high ratings on The Freedom Functions:

- Collaborative Relating
- Mixed Representative and Authoritarian Governance
- Entrepreneurial Enterprise

The good news was that, however "ugly" externally, the U.S.A. continued to relate collaboratively internally and with friends and neighbors. Moreover, the U.S.A. was convergent externally and internally with its path-finding Free Enterprise Mission. The bad news was attempting to project a democratic image in an authoritarian manner externally, while meaningful participative governance was dissembling internally.

U.S.A. 2008—The Consumer Culture

Once again, over the last century, the U.S.A. defined the emerging requirements of The Global Marketplace:

- Free Cultural Relating
- Participative Governance
- Entrepreneurial Enterprise

These are the requirements for entry into the 21st century marketplace. They also define the American Mission. Currently, the same subject-matter experts gave very different ratings in 2008.

Competitive Relating

In 2008, the U.S.A. is rated at level 2.0 on Cultural Relating (see Figure 9). This reflects her growing suspicion and hostility following the 9/11 terrorism attacks and her inability to translate "spy in the sky" intelligence data into meaningful "feet on the ground" information upon which she could base strong and operational security systems. In the absence of operational thinking systems, America writhed in agony and engaged in random, nonresponsive, and inappropriate initiatives emphasizing cultural competitiveness and the resultant cultural dependency reactions.

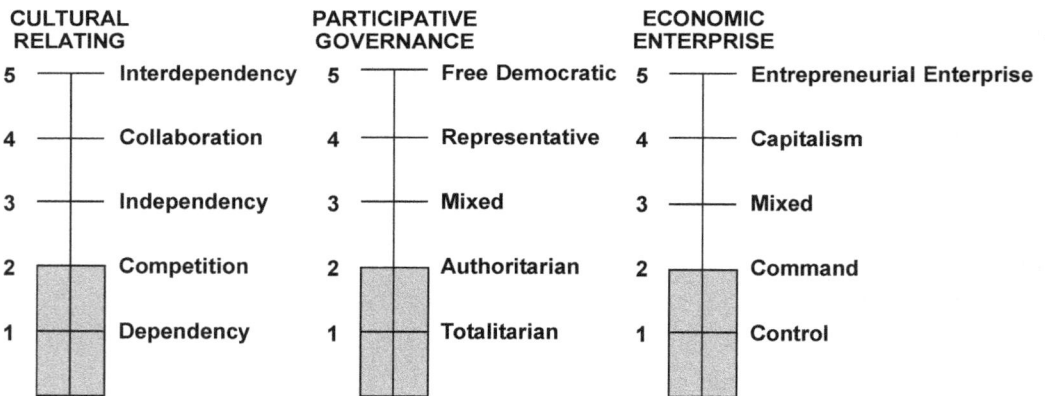

CULTURAL RELATING		PARTICIPATIVE GOVERNANCE		ECONOMIC ENTERPRISE	
5	Interdependency	5	Free Democratic	5	Entrepreneurial Enterprise
4	Collaboration	4	Representative	4	Capitalism
3	Independency	3	Mixed	3	Mixed
2	Competition	2	Authoritarian	2	Command
1	Dependency	1	Totalitarian	1	Control

Figure 9. U.S.A. Levels of the Freedom Functions (2008)

Authoritarian Governance

In 2008, the U.S.A. is rated at level 2.0 on Participative Governance (see again Figure 9), reflecting the increasing totalitarianism of the party in power and the reactive authoritarianism of the opposition: rather than being consulted as the constitutionally-mandated policy-makers, We the People, the citizens, feel imposed upon by the authoritarian inquisition: Either _____ or _____!

"Either you are a patriot or you're disloyal!"

"Either you are liberal or you're prejudiced!"

Command Economics

In 2008, the U.S.A. is rated at level 2.0 on Economic Enterprise (see again Figure 9), reflecting its shift in government sponsorship from a vision of an entrepreneurial-driven free enterprise system to government-reinforced multinational corporations, which by their very nature conduct "Command-and-Control Economics." In spite of their origins and support from American Freedom Functions, the Totalitarian Multinationals relate monopolistically and attempt to reduce their markets to dependency upon "Command-and-Control Strategies."

In summary, it is clear that America had indeed taken a "U-Turn on The Freedom Road." America received low ratings on Cultural Relating, Economic Enterprise, and Participative Governance. Under the administration of Bush II, the newly-minted Government-Reinforced Industrial-Military Complex (or "GRIM Complex") has placed America's citizenry as well as American destiny at risk.

- Competitive and Dependent Cultural Relating placed peace at risk—internally within the nation and externally in the Global Village!

- Authoritarian and Totalitarian Governance placed participation at risk—internally within the nation and externally in Global Governance and the Courts of Law and Justice!

- Command-and-Control Economics placed prosperity at risk—internally within the nation and externally in the Global Marketplace!

In transition, peace, participation, and prosperity are the historical functions of "The Producer Culture." Americans are placed at risk by "The Consumer-Driven Culture" that now accounts for 70 percent of GDP.

From Generativity to Degenerativity

Perhaps the greatest impact upon American generativity and innovation was the shift from a producer culture to a consumer culture. The producer-driven economy generated five decades of incredible economic growth. In turn, when converted, the consumer-driven economy led to the current economic bust.

How this came about is a complex tale of political economics. Why it came about is the more profound issue, for it had disastrous impact upon the American economy and its people.

Recall that America was rolling to victory in Europe and Asia when in 1944 the first Bretton Woods Conference was held. The result of this conference was to establish the American dollar as the universal standard for all currencies. The dollar, in turn, was backed by its own standard, "The Gold Standard."

The Generativity Curve

World War II had unleashed the awesome productivity of the American people. Indeed, as much as anything else, America's soldiers were successful because of America's accelerating manufacturing capacity, which provided the armaments and logistical support to the fighting men. It was a tribute to this very same morale, motivation, and mentality that warranted the Bretton Woods I concession. It tapped into the work ethic and fighting spirit of American men and women, many of whom were first generation Americans.

Indeed, it defined and reinforced a producer-driven economy that out-produced the world, not just in goods and services but in creativity and solutions. The American system was a "groove" for the producer mentality. In the 1950s, companies like IBM exemplified "The Golden Age of Industry" with "The GIC System":

- **Generators** made "breakthroughs" at The Watson Center.

- **Innovators** made "applications" at Advanced Systems Development.

- **Commercializers** made profits with their ubiquitous marketing arms.

The generators, innovators, and commercializers related together interdependently in "The GIC System." Each component had its own unique functions. Yet, all components were committed to integrating their individual contributions into the company mission. Their motto was "THINK!" Recognizing that all stood together or all fell apart, they prospered as the leaders of "The Golden Age of Business for America."

As may be viewed in Figure 10, the producer-driven economy, led by generators and innovators, led the market on an elevating and escalating curve of growth. The people prospered and, indeed, flourished in generating their own unique American culture exemplified by the following conditions:

- **Cultural relating** transformed America from a "boiling cauldron" to a "melting pot" and provided the human capital support for "The Production Machine."

- **Participative governance** transformed Americans from the dependent minions of autocratic Anglophiles to the enlightened citizens of a transparent and accountable government.

- **Free enterprise** economics transformed Americans from extensions of their own industrial machinery to entrepreneurial capitalists in a generative economy of their own making.

AMERICAN GDP

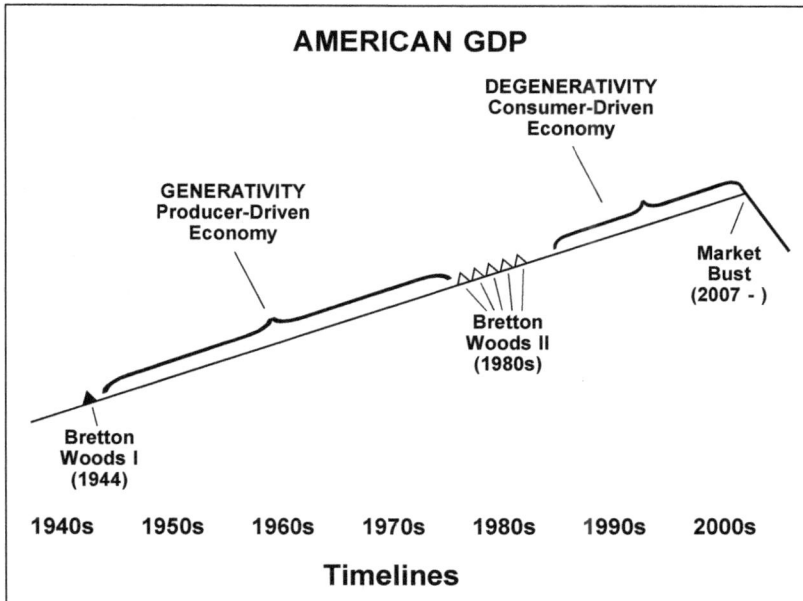

Figure 10. The Effects of Interventions upon Generativity

Degenerativity

Things were looking great when some of America's alleged leaders overstepped their political boundaries. During the 1980s, in their conflict with the Soviet Union for world domination, they began to negotiate deals with nations around the world. In the heat of passion, Kissinger's pragmatism replaced Reagan's idealism: in so doing, it transformed Reagan's divine mission into "a little for you and a little for me" diplomacy:

> Adopt democratic governance and defeat communism and you will
> grow rich as our trading partners.

There was only one problem—a huge problem! The countries of the world wanted to trade only if they had a positive trade balance. It was left to America to choose: between demonstrating and dominating; between leading and saving the world; between capitalism and ideology; between prosperity and "faux prosperity." America chose poorly!

In the 1980s and early 1990s, there were a series of conferences between America and its leading trading partners. Informally, these meetings may be labeled "Bretton Woods II," although American leaders ignored the same ideology they were exporting: the American citizenry did not participate in the nontransparent decision-making; the American people did not understand the cost of "The Free Enterprise Vision."

The sum of Bretton Woods II was this: America continues to trade at a deficit and its trading partners initiate to buy their debtor bonds. Initially Japan, and now China, have assumed the leadership role of creditor bond-buying nations. "It was a good deal for the peasants," our Ivy-League leaders concluded.

49

The net of the initiatives of Bretton Woods II was to transform American culture from a producer culture to a consumer culture. The "good deal" was that Americans could purchase things at the cheapest prices in the world and consume more than any people in the history of the world. All questions were answered with the basic Walmart question: "Do you like the prices, or what?"

The long-term problem was this: when we changed the culture, we changed the character of the American people. The older generations were confused and disoriented. Were we supposed to model ourselves after scientists, teachers, and mechanics who pursued knowledge and empowered expertise? Or were we supposed to model ourselves after businessmen and traders who pursued only profits and produced only cheap goods? The younger generations were to answer these questions.

Almost instantaneously, the younger generations were impacted by the "one-trial conditioning" of the ubiquitous media campaign: "Make more and pay less!" They bought whole-hog the assumptions of consumerism as the driving force in the marketplace. Indeed, they made it into the ethic of their generation. To be sure, they labeled it "The Consumer Ethic."

Some of us in the older generations lost contact with this new ethic. We thought that we had to learn some substance and produce something of value. We thought that we had to demonstrate that the way of American productivity was the best way: the healthiest way, the most civilized way, the most moral way in the sense of the Judaic Christian work ethic upon which this country was built. We believed that we would lead the world by producing—not by consuming!

Like "a shooting guard without a conscience," the younger generations applied the ethic "Buy!" It was the answer to every market explosion: "Buy!" Indeed, it was the answer that Bush II gave to the market depression: "Buy!" To be sure, "The New Buyology" is the answer we hear to our current economic depression: "Prop them up so they can buy things up."

It is the death gurgle of a dying civilization: "Buy!"

We desperately need a Bretton Woods III: to install the producer engine of economic growth; to drive consuming by producing; to generate possibilities and produce probabilities.

Chapter 5

"Generator, Innovator, Commercializer": Socioeconomic Generativity

For three decades, the "Entrepreneurial Capital" of the world has thrived in Silicon Valley, California, with the "Generation–Innovation–Venture Capital–Initial Public Offering (IPO) Cycle" generating new wealth, commercializing innovation, and creating new companies and industries while spinning off millions of new jobs. This "Cycle of Generativity" is self-perpetuating: entrepreneurs generate new ideas, form teams, innovate and plan, and promote the ideas to venture capitalists (VCs). In turn, VCs invest, "start-ups" perform, IPOs are offered. The cycle begins again with the profitability and reinvestment of the companies. The success of this engine in our economy is over, under assault by legislators and regulators who do not understand the fragile nature of Generativity. In the name of "fairness," all governmental agencies have put Generativity at risk.

These are the Generativity Functions in operation: the Generator generates "breakthrough ideas;" the Innovator transfers the ideas to the marketplace; the Commercializer commercializes the ideas to maximize profitability. These are the critical phases of Economic Generativity, the culminating mission of the Generativity Cycle.

This, then, is the Generativity Cycle. Beginning with Community Generativity, Individual and Organizational Generativity are nested in the community that is the generator of New Capital Development:

- **Marketplace capital** or positioning for comparative advantage

- **Organizational capital** or productive alignment with positioning

- **Human capital** or generative processing to implement alignment

- **Information capital** or information modeling to implement processing

- **Mechanical capital** or mechanical tooling to implement modeling

Together, these new capital ingredients provide the building blocks for Cultural Generativity.

In turn, Cultural Generativity is empowered by networks of Generative Communities capable of generating new capital. What holds these communities together are the freedom functions that culminate in Cultural Capital Development:

- **Cultural relating,** which relates the communities collaboratively and interdependently

- **Participative governance,** which empowers the communities to democratic and enlightened governance

- **Free enterprise,** which empowers the communities to entrepreneurial and capitalistic enterprise

51

Together, the freedom functions provide the foundation for the spiraling benefits of "The Pillars of Civilization"—peace, participation, and prosperity.

Finally, Economic Generativity is founded by networks of Generative Cultures. Economic Generativity culminates in Economic Capital Development:

- **Generativity,** which creates breakthrough ideas and architectures

- **Innovation**, which transfers these architectures into products and services dedicated to marketplace functions

- **Commercialization**, which markets and sells the products and services, yielding productivity and profitability in the marketplace

Together, these economic functions define the mission of a continuously changing and growing marketplace.

In sharp relief, then, the mission of Economic Generativity is very simple:

> Economic functions are achieved by cultural components that are empowered by community processes.

Together, all of these dimensions process interdependently and synergistically to generate explosions of wealth heretofore unknown to humankind.

The only real obstacles are those brought about by the reinforcement schedules of our consumer-driven culture:

- We have been positively rewarded to expect comfort and even luxury in our buying habits.

- We have been extinguished by neutral responses to our working habits.

- We have been negatively reinforced by punishments in our "producing initiatives."

In other words, our consumer-driven culture has inverted the reinforcement schedules for an economic recovery.

Clearly, we can already see that the socialistic system undermines the operation of the Generativity Cycle. After an average of hundreds of individual public offerings (IPOs) per year over the past three decades, there have been only six IPOs from Silicon Valley in 2008, or 2% of the filings of an average year. Our choices are clear:

- Assume a static marketplace and "teach our children Mandarin."

- Assume a changing marketplace and "teach our children Generativity!"

Generativity Positioning Systems

The Generativity Economy begins with positioning. Without positioning, the organization or economy cannot gain or maintain comparative advantage over others in the marketplace. Another way of saying this is that positioning differentiates our economy's unique contributions.

However, in today's world, we cannot talk about positioning as simply differentiating ourselves from our competitors. Competition is the function of static resources and independent attitudes. Independence and competition, as we once practiced it, will not work anymore.

Today, we position as interdependent partnerships with nearly everyone: customers, customers of customers, vendors, suppliers, and, yes, even entities that we might still consider "competitors." Collaboration is the function of interdependence. Today, positioning differentiates our interdependent collaborative contributions.

All business policymakers will concede that the success of a corporation begins with its positioning in the marketplace. Yet all of these top executives also will admit that they were never taught "positioning." Many employ "legacy positioning" by "sticking to the knitting" and adding new, related product and service lines. Others employ "existential positioning" by "cleaning the slate" and entering those markets with highly leveraged opportunities. There are many other strategies in between these extremes—some very personal and idiosyncratic. But none are systematic in positioning their corporations in the marketplace!

One of the great ironies of business is this: we know so much about the technologies we employ to produce our product and service lines, but so little about the technologies of the business practices that determine the success or failure of our businesses. That is partly the reason why our business successes are random and seldom replicated.

Increasingly, top executives are driven by fast-changing marketplace requirements. As breakthroughs evolve through the rapid market life cycle, executives must address the derivative requirements of these breakthroughs. Marketplace requirements are not simply based upon corporate values or executive choices. The marketplace itself "speaks" and its requirements must be understood. With this understanding, corporations take an index of their capacities to address these requirements. Corporations need technological capabilities in precisely the same areas as the requirements.

To enable the corporation to mobilize its technological capacities to address its marketplace requirements, executives must understand the processes of marketplace positioning. All positioning to enhance corporate capacities to meet marketplace requirements is accompanied by implications for placement in the life cycle of the market.

We must remember: no organization is an independent entity. Our organizations are inextricably linked in generating the "New Market Life Cycle," from generativity and innovation through commercialization to commoditization and attenuation. Marketplace positioning must relate customer requirements with producer technologies, all within the context of the New Market Life Cycle.

Three points are particularly important here:

- **First, understanding the requirements of the marketplace is crucial to positioning.** In effect, marketplace requirements are the values of the marketplace. This is analogous to career placement: we have our values, and the job has its own values; the values of the job become the requirements of the person. In marketplace positioning, the marketplace values become the organization's requirements. Our external mission is to position our organizations to meet or to exceed these marketplace requirements.

- **Second, gaining the technological capability to meet marketplace requirements is our internal mission.** This, too, is analogous to career placement: if we have the right skills, knowledge, and attitudes, we can get the job. Mobilizing technological capacity to meet marketplace requirements is the essential function of the organization.

- **Third, how we address the requirements of the marketplace with our organizational capacities has implications for our placement in the market life cycle.** Beginning with generativity, possibilities are transformed into marketplace applications by innovation, and culminate in profitable products and services by commercialization. An interdependent partnering relationship among these three phases of the market life cycle is essential for powerful positioning in the marketplace.

Technological capabilities and marketplace requirements are both "moving targets" in the New Market Life Cycle. Whatever economy *best understands the market's requirements, builds its technological capabilities, and partners across the market life cycle* is taking the first step toward becoming a "Generativity Organization."

Armed with the Ideational Image products of our Generative Processing, we may now position our organizations or economies in the marketplace. Our most powerful positioning is to be able to do something no other entity can do.

Generative–Innovative positioning was the historic positioning of the American economy in the latter part of the 20th century. Today, the same positioning requires that we offer "virtual off-the-shelf products" that customers may choose to have tailored to their needs.

The prepotent breakthrough model is the Generativity Positioning and Processing System™ or GPPS™ (see Figure 11). As may be noted, GPPS™ represents and implements Generative–Innovator Positioning in the Marketplace at the highest levels as follows:

Generative Positioning Functions are accomplished by **Cultural Capital Development** (CCD') empowered by **Community Capital Development** (CCD) processes.

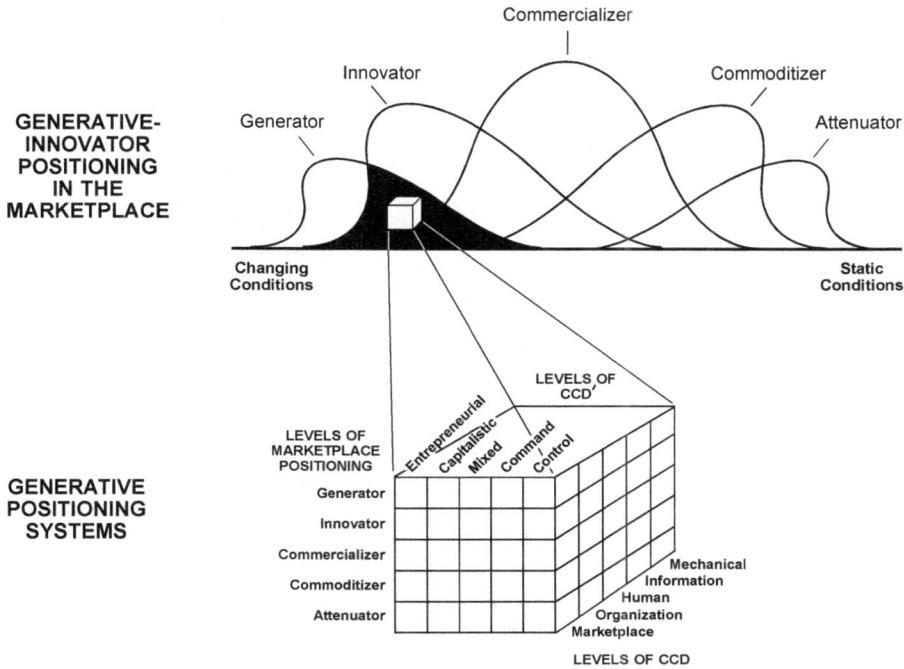

Figure 11. The Generativity Positioning and Processing System™
Representation in the Marketplace

The most critical function of this GPPS™ source cell is implementing the Require-ments–Capacities Matrix: the capacities of the organization are compared against the requirements for Generative–Innovative Positioning in the marketplace. Clearly, Genera-tivity Positioning is going to require the highest levels of new capital development to establish and continuously maintain positioning.

In GPPS™, the customer may select, from potentially an infinite array, those prod-ucts that are (1) most closely tailored to meet the customer's values, and (2) for which the customers are empowered by tailored capacities to meet the product's requirements for managing.

For example, the customer may view electronic representations of all kinds of products—homes, cars, equipment—via Computer-Assisted Design. The customers may then select and "tailor" those products to meet their needs.

The generative marketplace of the future will be driven by the Generativity Solution—the generativity of breakthrough initiatives and architectural designs (see Figure 12). Anything of value that can be conceived can be achieved in Generativity Positioning and Processing Systems™ of new capital development.

- MCD or Continuous Marketplace Positioning for Comparative Advantage
- OCD or Continuous Organization Alignment with Marketplace Positioning
- HCD or Generative Human Processing to implement Organizational Alignment
- ICD or Schematic Information Modeling to reflect Generative Human Processing
- mCD or Operational Mechanical Tooling to implement Schematic Information Modeling

55

MCD

COMPONENTS

FUNCTIONS
Policy
Executive
Management
Supervision
Delivery

Generator

Innovator

Commercializer

Commoditizer

Attenuator

PROCESSES
Production
Technology
Resources
Marketing
Leadership

OCD

Leadership
Marketing
Resources
Technology
Production

Policy

Executive

Management

Supervision

Delivery

Outputting
Planning
Processing
Inputting
Goaling

HCD

Goaling
Inputting
Processing
Planning
Outputting

Leadership

Marketing

Resources

Technology

Production

Conceptual
Operational
Dimensional
Vectorial
Phenomenal

ICD

Phenomenal
Vectorial
Dimensional
Operational
Conceptual

Goaling

Inputting

Processing

Planning

Outputting

Standards
Conditions
Processes
Components
Functions

mCD

Functions
Components
Processes
Conditions
Standards

Phenomenal

Vectorial

Dimensional

Operational

Conceptual

Implementation
Steps
Tasks
Instructions
Programs

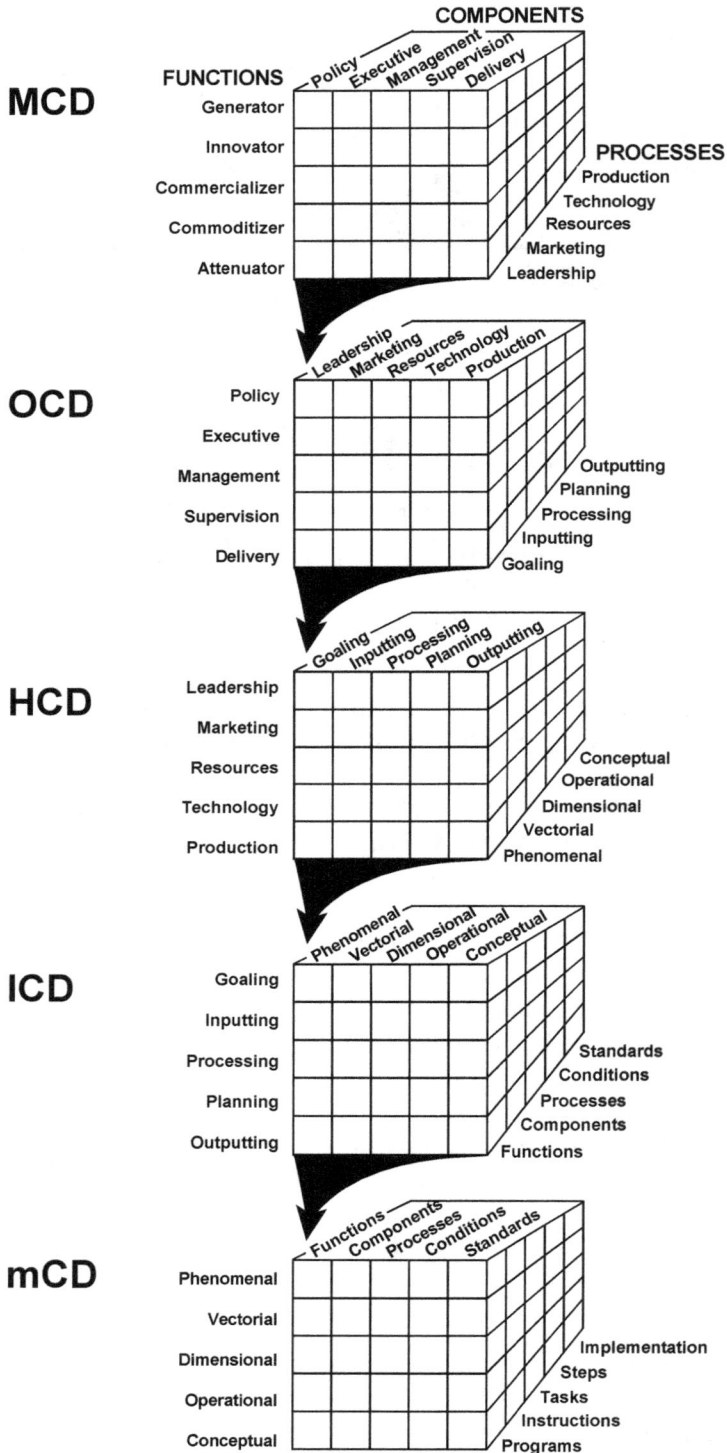

Figure 12. New Capital Development Systems

The actual design and assembly of the products will be "farmed out" to "MOHIMs" for the New Capital Development Systems, just as OEMs or Original Equipment Manufacturers currently organize their production efforts.

The paradigm shift to GPPS™ requires that all NCD Components contribute to the substance of the products being produced and delivered. The criteria of measurement revolve around increasing the "size of the pie" rather than redistributing the "sizes of the pieces."

In this context, we will have once again placed Americans back in the leadership role:

- The American learners with expansive acquisition of operational knowledge and skills

- The American workers with elevating levels of applications and transfers in producing products and delivering services

- The American entrepreneurs with escalating levels of ideational generativity and "commanding heights" positioning generating wealth

- The American citizens with accelerating levels of enlightenment and participation in governance and politics

- The American leaders with potentially infinite levels of continuous interdependent processing in all areas of policy-making

In other terms, we will have a fulfillment of Human Generativity, reinvigoration of the New Capitalism, and a Renaissance of Possibilities Civilization.

Just as the organizational leaders on Main Street and Wall Street need to learn the ingredients of corporate growth, so do the national leaders in America need to learn the ingredients of "Real Socioeconomic Growth."

Just as the underclass people marginalized by "The Cycle of Social Failure" need to learn how to become productive individually, so do those marginalized by "The Cycle of Financial Failure" need to learn to perform productively and profitably in our times.

Rather than to pit Main Street versus Wall Street versus Constitution Avenue, we must all learn to become generative in entrepreneurial ways where each grows so that all have the opportunity to grow.

In transition, the Generativity Solution empowers us to solve all human crises. The Generativity Solution is "The Human Solution."

Chapter 6

"The Human Universe":
Generativity Civilization Designs

In generating our Community Capital Development (CCD) designs, we then begin with the Individual Generativity Matrix. As illustrated below (Figure 13), the Human Processing (HP) factors are dedicated to inductively processing the Information Representing (IR) factors. Potentially, this matrix may define the boundaries of the "Human Universe" in which we are processing. This Individual Generativity Matrix will tell us the effects of each level of each factor upon every level of both factors.

Human Processing (HP)

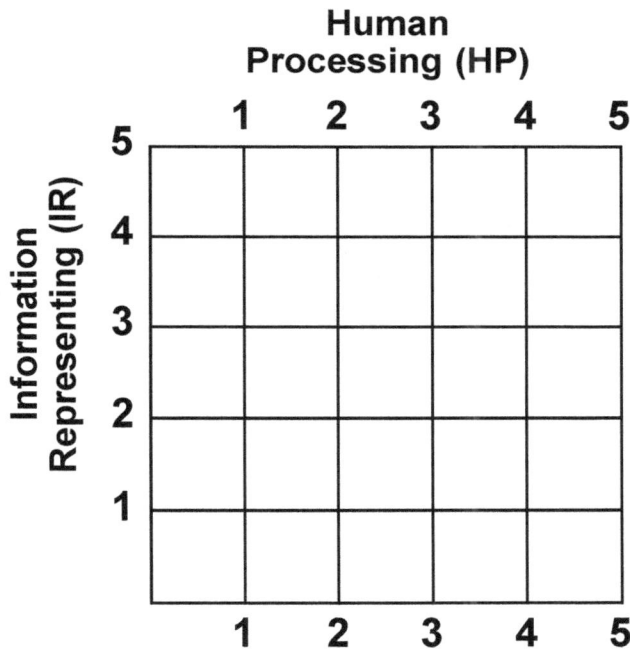

Figure 13. The Individual Generativity Matrix (Inductive)

In the next image (Figure 14), the human and information factors are dedicated to higher-order organizational functions:

OCD functions are achieved by HCD components enabled by ICD processes.

As may be viewed, the higher-order functions (**OCD**) are empowered by lower-order components (**HCD**) enabled by **ICD** processes:

Legend (Figure 14)

OCD		**HCD**		**ICD**	
M —	Marketplace	R^1 —	Relating	S^1 —	Sentences
O —	Organization	R^2 —	Representing	S^2 —	Systems
H —	Human	R^3 —	Reasoning by Exploring	S^3 —	Schematics
I —	Information	R^4 —	Reasoning by Understanding	S^4 —	Social Schematics
m —	Mechanical	R^5 —	Reasoning by Acting	S^5 —	Spatial Schematics

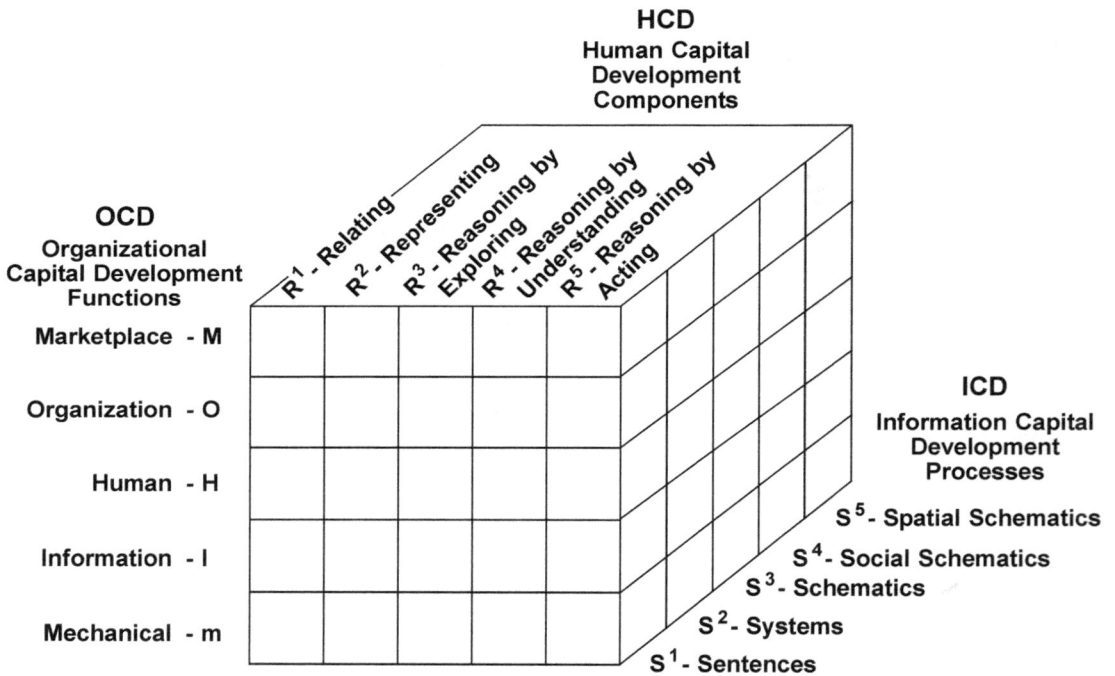

Figure 14. Individual Generativity Model

These Individual Generativity Models (**HCD ↔ ICD**) may be represented developmentally (see Figure 15). As may be noted, the evolving Organizational Capital Development Models (**OCD**) have elevating requirements for performance of organizational functions:

OCD Legend (Figure 15)

Capital Development (OCD)

MCD = Marketplace CD
OCD = Organization CD
HCD = Human CD
ICD = Information CD
mCD = Mechanical CD

Components

R^1 = Relating for Goaling
R^2 = Representing for Inputting
R^3 = Reasoning for Exploring
R^4 = Reasoning for Understanding
R^5 = Reasoning for Acting

Functions

M = Market
O = Organization
H = Human
I = Information
m = Mechanical

Processes

S^5 = Spatial Schematics (Phenomena)
S^4 = Social Schematics (Vectorial)
S^3 = Schematics (Dimensional)
S^2 = Systems (Operational)
S^1 = Sentences (Conceptual)

INDIVIDUAL GENERATIVITY MODELS

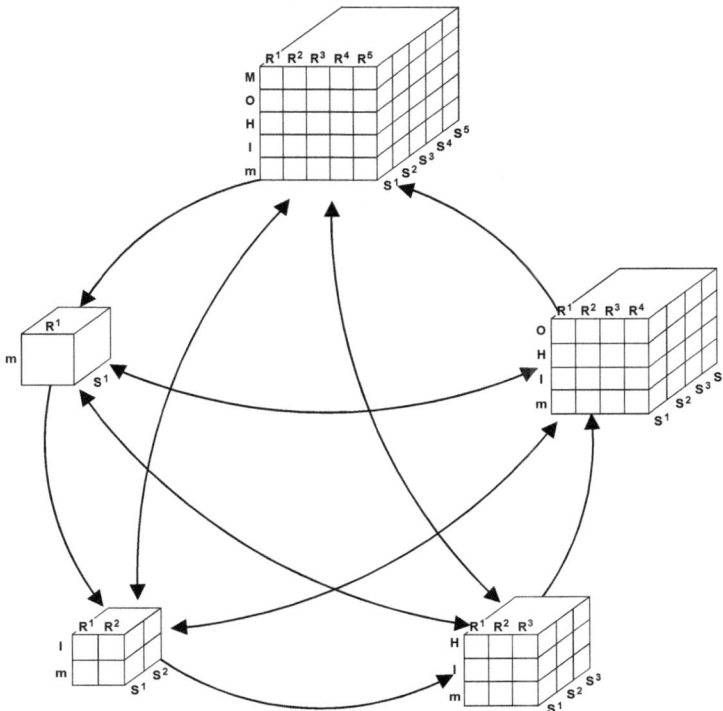

Figure 15. Individual Generativity Models Dedicated to Organizational Capital Development (OCD) Functions

Just as individuals evolve developmentally, so do organizations evolve in terms of accomplishing higher-order functions. In Figure 16, we may view the organizations originating from a single mechanical cell (**mCD**) all the way to multidimensional cells required for positioning in the marketplace (**MCD**):

OCD Legend (Figure 16)

Organizational Capital Development

MCD = Marketplace
OCD = Organization
HCD = Human
ICD = Information
mCD = Mechanical

Components

L = Leadership
M = Marketing
R = Resource Integration
T = Technology
P = Production

Functions

P = Policy
E = Executive
M = Management
S = Supervision
D = Delivery

Processes

G = Goaling
I = Information
P = Processing
P = Planning
O = Outputting

ORGANIZATIONAL GENERATIVITY MODELS

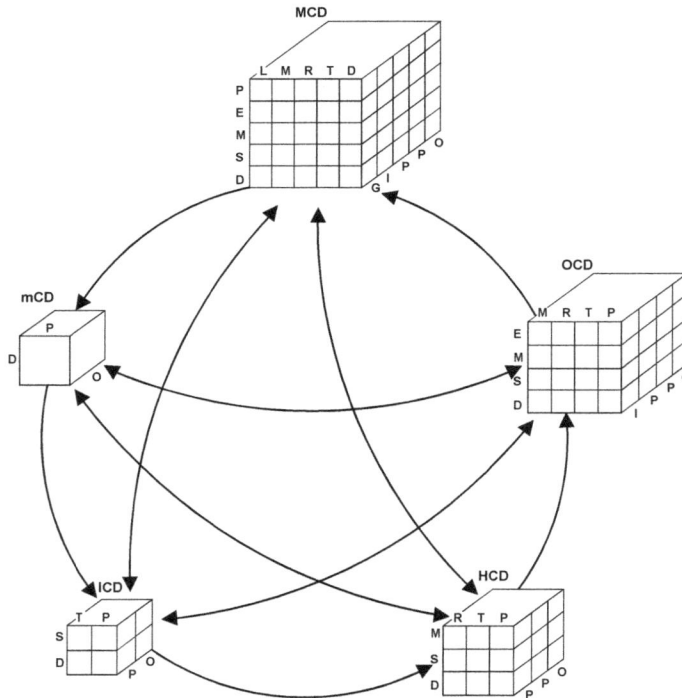

Figure 16. Organization Capital Development (OCD) Models

As the organization evolves developmentally, then, the requirements for accomplishing organizational functions evolve developmentally. In Figure 17, the **"Source Cells"** of **OCD** are illustrated as the sources of **HCD** and **ICD** requirements:

ICD Legend (Figure 17)

Organizational Capital Development (OCD)

MCD = Marketplace CD
OCD = Organization CD
HCD = Human CD
ICD = Information CD
mCD = Mechanical CD

Components

R^1 = Relating for Goaling
R^2 = Representing for Inputting
R^3 = Reasoning for Exploring
R^4 = Reasoning for Understanding
R^5 = Reasoning for Acting

Functions

M = Market
O = Organization
H = Human
I = Information
m = Mechanical

Processes

S^5 = Spatial Schematics (Phenomena)
S^4 = Social Schematics (Vectorial)
S^3 = Schematics (Dimensional)
S^2 = Systems (Operational)
S^1 = Sentences (Conceptual)

OCD MODEL

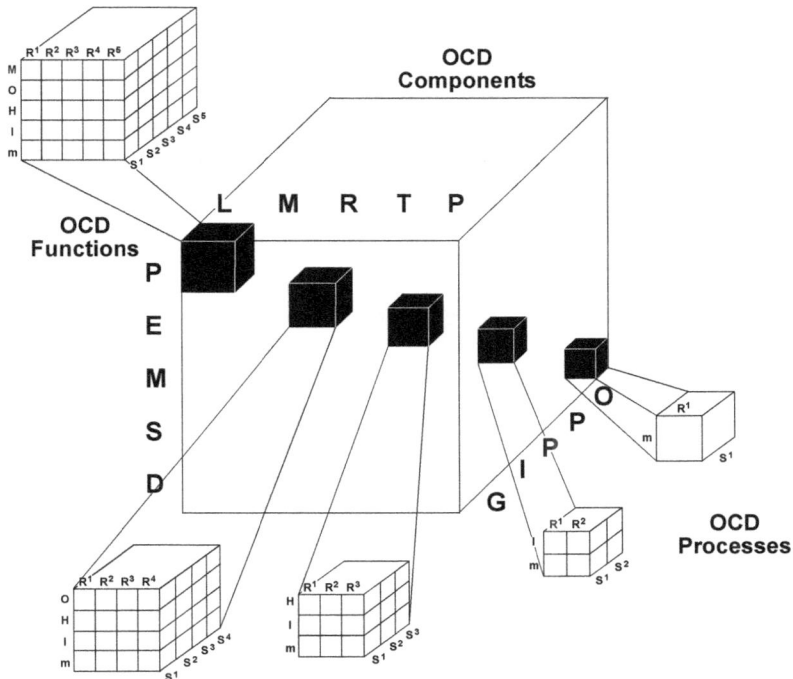

Figure 17. Individual Generativity Models Dedicated to Organizational Capital Development

63

As the organizations evolve developmentally in the community, they have increasing requirements for human and information generativity. As may be viewed in Figure 18, in Community Capital Development (**CCD**), increasing levels of organization generativity range from the one-celled home (**mCD**) through to the multi-celled businesses positioning themselves in the marketplace (**MCD**):

CCD Legend (Figure 18)

Community Capital Development (CCD)

MCD	=	Marketplace CD
OCD	=	Organization CD
HCD	=	Human CD
ICD	=	Information CD
mCD	=	Mechanical CD

HCD Components

R^1	=	Relating for Goaling
R^2	=	Representing for Inputting
R^3	=	Reasoning for Exploring
R^4	=	Reasoning for Understanding
R^5	=	Reasoning for Acting

OCD Functions

M	=	Market
O	=	Organization
H	=	Human
I	=	Information
m	=	Mechanical

ICD Processes

S^5	=	Spatial Schematics (Phenomena)
S^4	=	Social Schematics (Vectorial)
S^3	=	Schematics (Dimensional)
S^2	=	Systems (Operational)
S^1	=	Sentences (Conceptual)

OCD Components

L	=	Leadership
M	=	Marketing
R	=	Resource Integration
T	=	Technology
P	=	Production

OCD Processes

G	=	Goaling
I	=	Inputting
P	=	Processing
P	=	Planning
O	=	Outputting

CCD MODEL

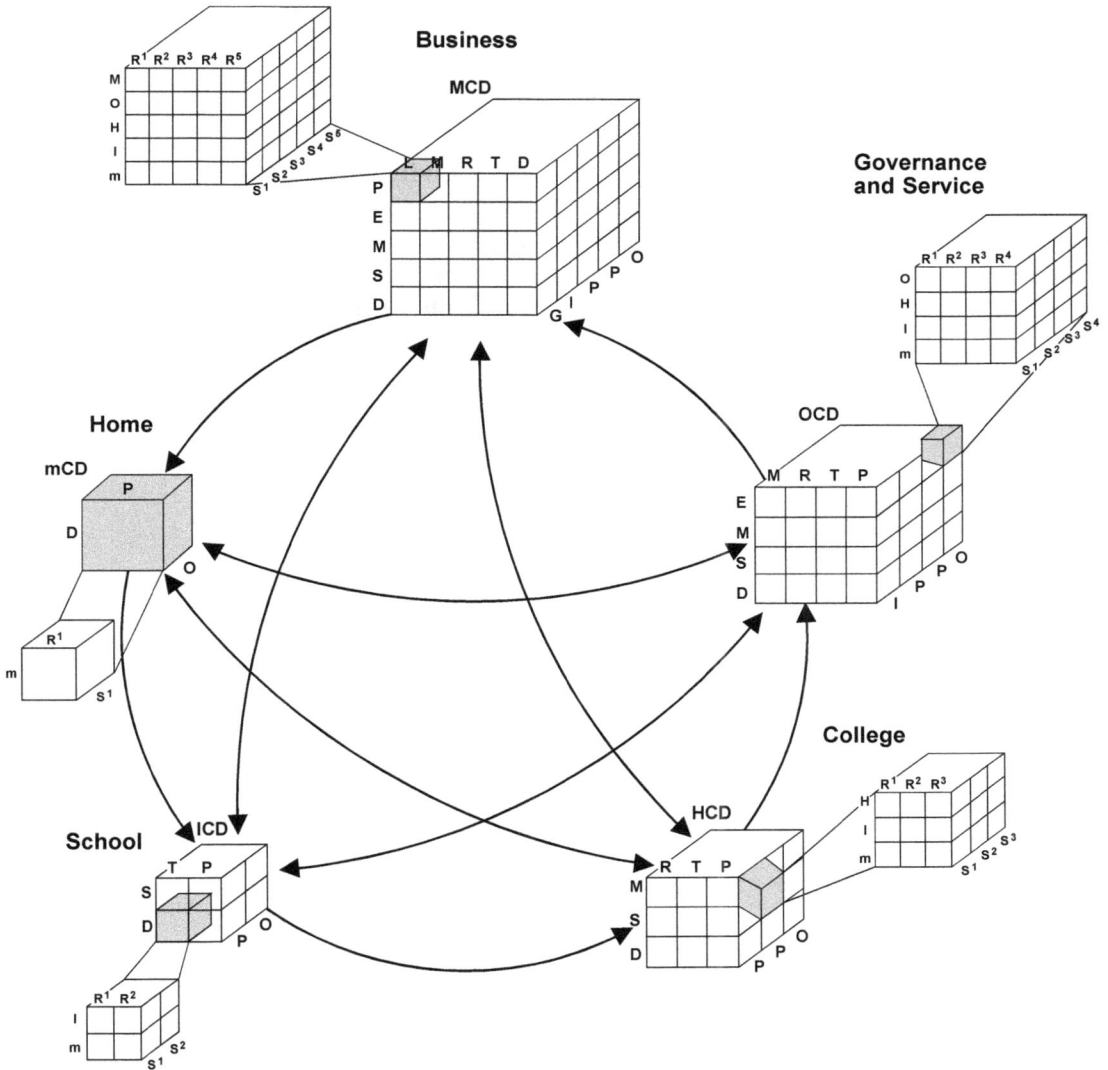

Figure 18. Organization Generativity Models Dedicated to Community Capital Development (CCD) Model

In transition, each level of generativity empowers the higher level of capital development as follows:

- Individual Generativity → **HCD** → **ICD**

- Individual Generativity → **OCD**

- Organizational Generativity → **CCD**

As has been demonstrated, the core of all generativity is individual generativity. Indeed, individual generativity accounts for as much as 85% of organizational productivity and, in turn, of community productivity. It is **HCD ↔ ICD,** which defines the synergistic growth of all phenomena: each grows as the other grows; all grow as generativity becomes prepotent. Unlike all other human factors, generativity is necessary and sufficient for all human endeavors.

Chapter 7

"The Civilized Culture":
The Socioeconomic Outcomes

Fast-forward to the modal outcomes of the HCD project for 400 male and female family profiles (Table 2).

Table 2. Comparison of HCD Levels Before and After Intervention

INDEX	PROFILE A (Before 1968)	PROFILE B (After 1988)
Employment	Unemployed	Employed
Education	7th grade	1 year college
Human Relations	Nonattentive	Responsive
Family Relations	Nonattentive	Responsive
Drug/Alcohol Dependency	Dependency	No use
Antisocial Behavior	Recent arrests	No crime
Community Contributions	None	Continuous contributions

For individuals trained for task performance on entry-level jobs, their performance was truly remarkable. Together, they told the story of HCD. Their graduation theme was "The Impossible Dream."

More important than anything else is the index of recidivism. For 200 ex-convicts over 20 years, none were convicted for another crime: Zero Percent Rate of Recidivism!

Never before in human history have so many produced such low results (70% to 85% recidivism is common for most programs)! Indeed, we concluded that we had generated a Civilized Culture: one based on healthy values, attitudes, skills, and knowledge.

Human Generativity

If we view Figure 19, we may see the performance indicators for **Human and Information Capital Development (HCD ↔ ICD).** While the 100% outcomes may appear inflated, they are not! Success on these indices was built into their participation in the curricula of the **HCD Project** (Figure 19):

MCD — There is no reason for an unemployed person to participate other than to become employed.

OCD — There is no reason for a powerless citizen to participate other than to become empowered in participating in government.

HCD — There is no reason for an uneducated learner to participate other than to become educated.

ICD — There is no reason for an irresponsible parent to participate other than to share in his or her child's learning and growth.

mCD — There is no reason for a socially impotent parent to participate other than to rear his or her child facilitatively and, in so doing, become a **"potent reinforcer"** of children.

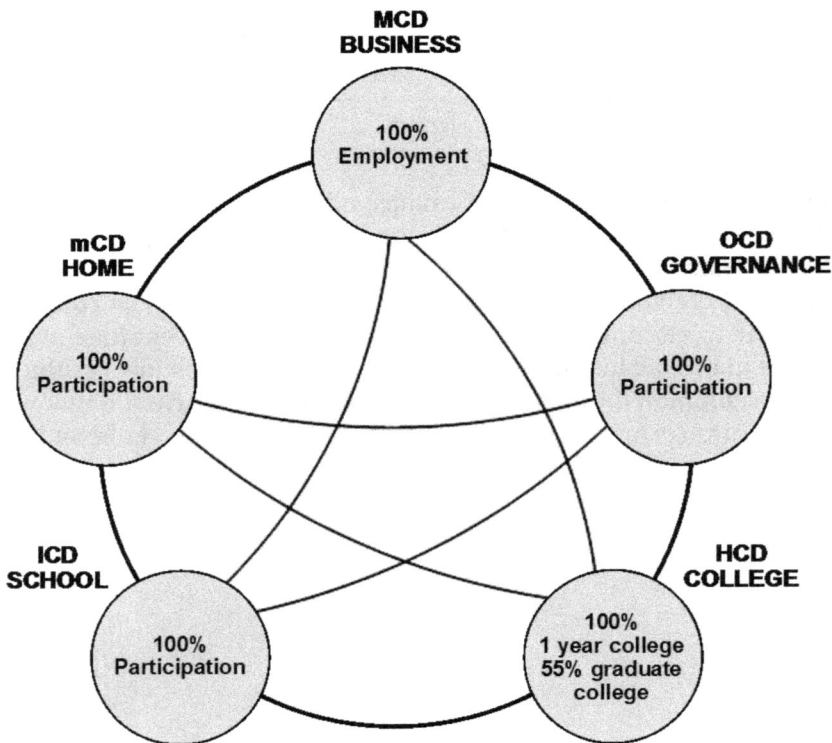

Figure 19. Human Generativity → Community Generativity

Information Generativity

Perhaps more important than the **Human Generativity** outcomes were the **Information Generativity** outcomes as a source of **Community Generativity** (Figure 20):

MCD — Repositioned for **IT** in the Information Age marketplace.

OCD — Realigned for community entry into the **IT** era.

HCD — Rededicated to thinking in human generativity terms.

ICD — Rededicated to learning in information generativity terms.

mCD — Rededicated to facilitative child-rearing in **"How Things Work!"**

Altogether, these policies were summarized as **The Springfield Miracle.** [*] As these programs were transferred to Boston, they became known as **The Massachusetts Miracle,** an expression that Governor Michael Dukakis adopted as the theme of his 1987–1988 campaign for the presidency.

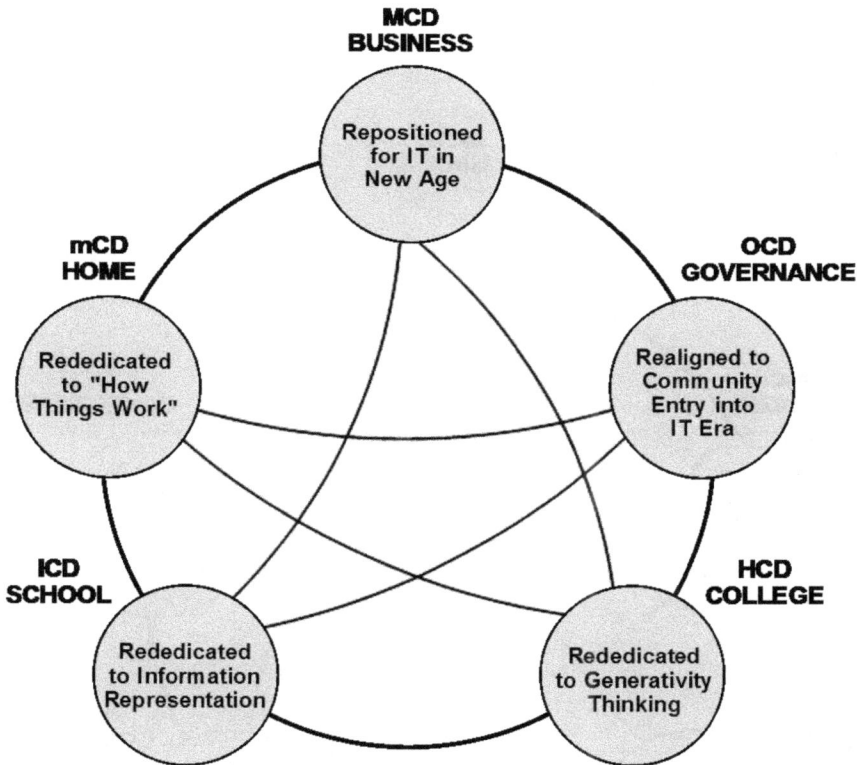

Figure 20. Information Generativity → Community Generativity

---

[*] Nocera, J. The Springfield Miracle. *Newsweek.* June 6, 1988, pp. 45–48.

Graduate Generativity

Now we can turn to more personal data for exemplary performers at the clinical or anecdotal level (Figure 21):

MCD — Bob ("Sephus") Jackson, former War Minister of BANG ("Black African Nascent Group"), who now is the entrepreneurial owner of businesses for which he recruits and trains "kids who were thugs like me"

OCD — Ray Jordan, former Massachusetts State Senator who chaired the House Ways and Means Committee that passed legislation for Social Casework Technicians who performed as functional professionals in Springfield

HCD — June Glenn, who received her degree from Massachusetts Institute of Technology and led the Strong Black Woman's Group

ICD — Maurita Bledsoe and Ron Carroll, who were co-leaders of the Human Relations Specialist Program responsible for resolving many school-community crises, including the Technical High School Riot

mCD — Bill Clinton, who became Program Director for the HRD Center for Counseling and Training working proactively with troubled families

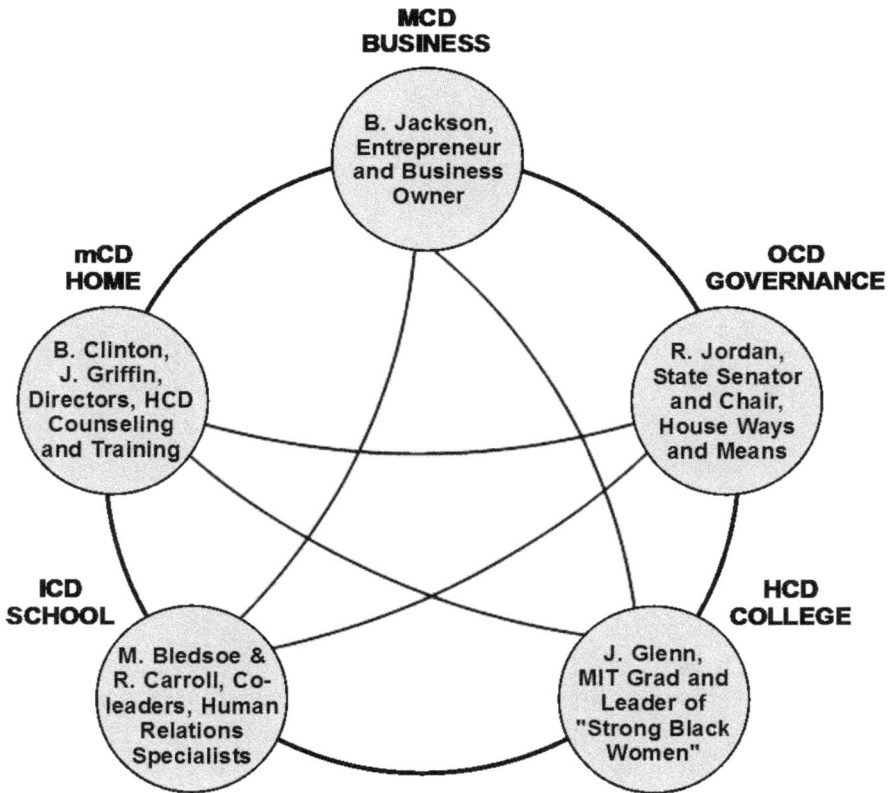

Figure 21. Exemplary Graduates in Community Generativity

Post-Graduate Generativity

Now we may turn to personal and anecdotal data on exemplars who went on to post-graduate studies (Figure 22):

MCD — Walt Reardon, MBA, Vice President of Massachusetts Mutual Life Insurance Company, who transformed Public Relations into Corporate–Community Relations

OCD — Robert Jennings, Director of Recreation, who established networks of youth leagues and inspired the building of the Girl's Club

HCD — Dr. George Banks, who, after taking his degrees at Harvard and S.U.N.Y., became a consultant to the Pentagon on Racial Relations

ICD — Rev. Bryant Robinson, who took graduate degrees in HRD and Religion before becoming Assistant Superintendent of Education in Springfield, and who is now Bishop of the Macedonian Church of Jesus Christ

mCD — Dr. Karen Banks, who took her graduate degrees in psychology before becoming a nationwide consultant to colleges and communities of early childhood education.

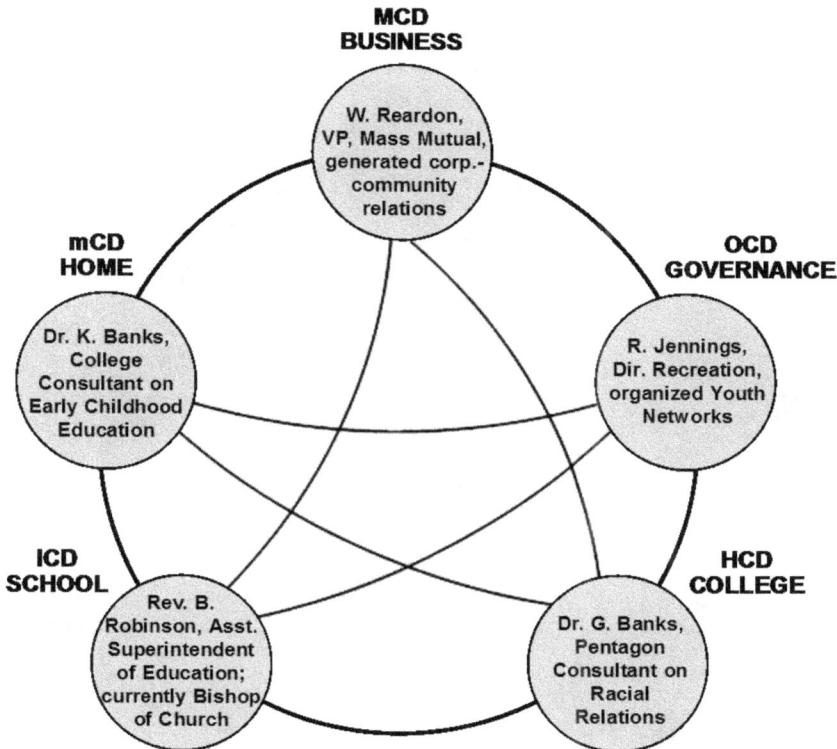

Figure 22. Exemplary Post-Graduates in Community Generativity

Sponsor Generativity

Finally, we get to acknowledge the contributions of exemplary sponsors to Community Generativity (Figure 23):

MCD — Jim Martin and Ben Jones, CEOs of Mass Mutual and Monarch Life Insurance Companies who, influenced by Dick Sprinthall, financed the HCD Project as a "righteous cause"

OCD — Captain Dan Shea of the police department, who monitored the HCD Project as a "guardian"

HCD — Harry Courniotes, President, American International College, who opened the doors to sponsor and credential Year 1 of the HCD Project

ICD — Louis Frayser, Director of Springfield Action Commission (**SAC**) and Roger Williams, Director, Concentrated Employment Program (**CEP**) who opened the doors to the HCD Project's "New Careers" program

mCD — Bruce Bowen, Director of Springfield Social Casework, who supervised the extraordinary Social Casework Technician Program, which impacted every home and family in the community.

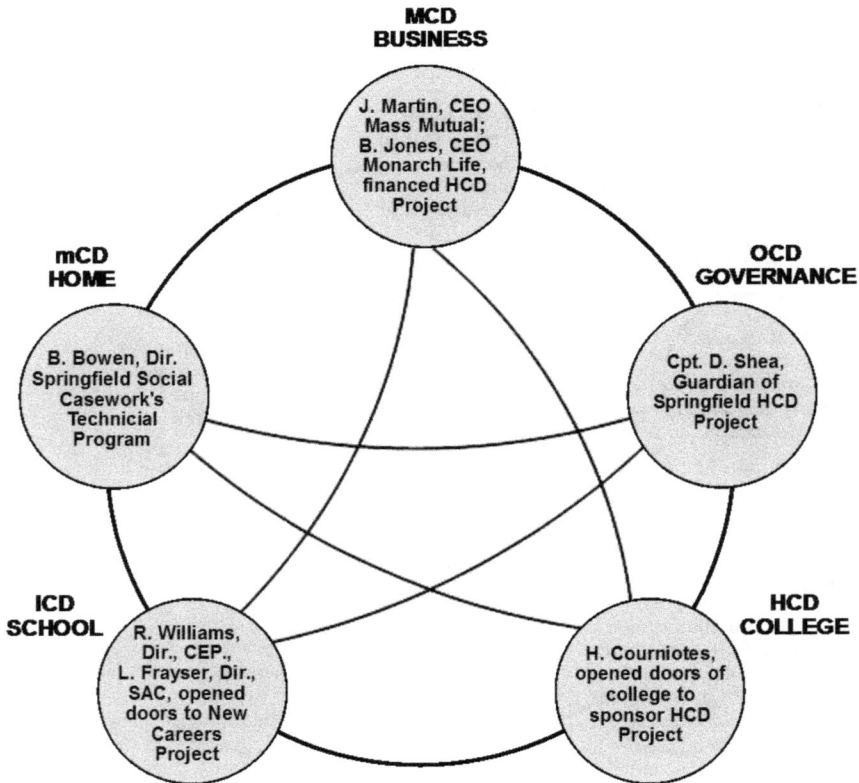

MCD BUSINESS

J. Martin, CEO Mass Mutual; B. Jones, CEO Monarch Life, financed HCD Project

mCD HOME

B. Bowen, Dir. Springfield Social Casework's Technicial Program

OCD GOVERNANCE

Cpt. D. Shea, Guardian of Springfield HCD Project

ICD SCHOOL

R. Williams, Dir., CEP., L. Frayser, Dir., SAC, opened doors to New Careers Project

HCD COLLEGE

H. Courniotes, opened doors of college to sponsor HCD Project

Figure 23. Exemplary Sponsors in Community Generativity

In Transition

These are just a sample of the many hundreds of participants and tens of leaders and contributors. They transformed Springfield from "The City of Homes" into "The City of Communities."

Most central to the success of the HCD Project were the commitments of the following professionals:

- Dr. Richard C. Sprinthall, who formulated the original interdependent design, relating the private sector to the marginalized communities, and housed it at A.I.C., where he became Dean of College of Education and Psychology.

- Dr. Andrew H. Griffin who, as community leader, led the integration with the private sector for employment and the college for education. He later became Assistant Superintendent of Education for the State of Washington, which led the nation in student retention and SAT performance.

- Dr. Bernard G. Berenson, who became the academic and research leader of the HCD Graduate Program as well as Director of the first Center for Human Capital Development.

Together, we converged upon one prepotent principle of human effectiveness and social justice: Continuous Interdependent Processing.

The rationale for integrating the modifier "Socio" with "Economic" is an attempt to generate an equitable distribution of prosperity derived from productivity. In fact, we were able to achieve this balance. Before they retired, the hundreds of minority graduates of the HCD Project surpassed the majority members in both employment and income.

Having established this principle of socioeconomic prosperity, I want to reassert my belief in the opportunity for upward mobility in The American Meritocracy.

- As great as the disparity was between the minority graduates and the majority population, the gap was greater with the minority post-graduates who went on to get advanced degrees and growth experiences.

- As great as this gap was between the post-graduates and graduates, the accomplishments were still greater for the sponsors.

There appears to be a confirmable hypothesis here. This is not a "zero-sum" game. Rather, it is a real-life experience of the geometric effects of generativity:

Generativity begets Possibilities

Those who benefitted most were those who were most prepared to grow. Put another way:

Those who grew the most were those who gave the most—and had the skills to do so!

In so doing, the **"Givers"** discovered **"The Basic Principle of Life:"**

The only reason to live is to grow!

It is with this learning that I have dedicated this work to Captain Dan Shea of the Springfield Police, serving his life-long mission **"To save and protect,"** he now serves his **"after-life"** mission:

To protect and extend.

Profoundly, it is from exemplars such as Dan Shea that I have learned the guiding principles of my own life:

Give all!

Ask none!

Have fun!

It's the interdependent culture, Dan!

Chapter 8

The McLean Project: From Community to Culture to Socioeconomics

In the wee hours immediately after the election of the country's first African American president, three white men crept up and burned a newly built African American church. This was their response to intrusion into sacred white territory.

As Bishop Bryant Robinson watched his beloved Macedonia Church of God in Christ burn to the ground, he concluded: "Rebuild!"

On September 25, 2011, nearly three years after the burning, Bishop Robinson celebrated the re-opening of his reconstructed 20,000 square foot church: "Reborn!"

People from all over the Springfield, Massachusetts community attended including its police force en masse.

Forty-five years earlier, Bryant was one of the graduates of the HRD program. And Dr. Andrew H. Griffin, Dr. Richard Sprinthall, and myself embraced him with all our love and respect. Like the ugly duckling, born anew as a beautiful swan, we were too happy to be proud.

This story does not conclude with the miraculous rebirth of the spirituality of a church that offers only love and hope, for Rev. Robinson brought a lot of other people with him into "the rapture!"

One of them I knew very well, since he also had been a product of our very intense HRD training program.

Minister of War, Deacon of Peace

Robert Jackson was a school drop-out and unemployed street thug when we met him. His friends called him Sephus, the Biblical "god of savagery." And Sephus lived up to his nickname!

As the minister of war of The Black American Nascent Group (BANG), in the 1960s, Sephus was a formidable terrorist leader who was always calling for "war unto death!" When I asked what BANG stood for, Sephus answered threateningly as he feigned a gun with his finger:

"What you think it mean, man?"

"Bye bye, whitey!"

Now Sephus stood in the front of Rev. Robinson's cavernous church. He was a deacon and greeted us with embraces as we rotated around to make our contributions. The third time, I said quietly to him:

"See, you the man!"

He answered reflexively:

"Dr. Carkhuff, you don't know how much that means to me!"

We met later and talked. It became clear to me that we had not simply run a community development program. We had conducted a cultural change program. He was now a Minister of Peace!

Moreover, Sephus was a Minister of Productivity. He owned several entrepreneurial businesses. In his own words:

"I now employ thugs like I was and help them to see the light!"

This is the point. What makes us think that we can con three billion or more members of newly developing countries and cultures to connect through the Internet without resolving these other potentially incendiary issues?

How do we expect to develop software and humanware that does not empower the new user to design and develop his or her own places of living, learning, and working based upon their own personal and spiritual values?

Was not Springfield's welfare of the 1960s the preparation for Global Welfare in the 2020s? (See the websites for **TheMcLeanProject.com** and its products* **).

---

 * **The McLeanProject.com**

Carkhuff GenerativityLibrary.com

My Takeaway

My "takeaway" from a lifetime of work in Generativity Solutions is that the American economy faces schizophrenic obstacles to recovery:

- As consumers, they lack employment and confidence in the market.

- As producers, they lack generativity and confidence in their ability to lead the market.

By far, the greatest obstacle is for Americans to ignite and elevate their generative functions. This means that putting the consumers back on their feet is, at best, a transitional mission. Empowering the producers with generativity vision and systems is the longer-term, overriding mission.

The "Generativity Stimulus Package" will reignite American ideation and entrepreneurial leadership. It defines the effective ingredients of "The New Economic Paradigm" (see Figure 24).

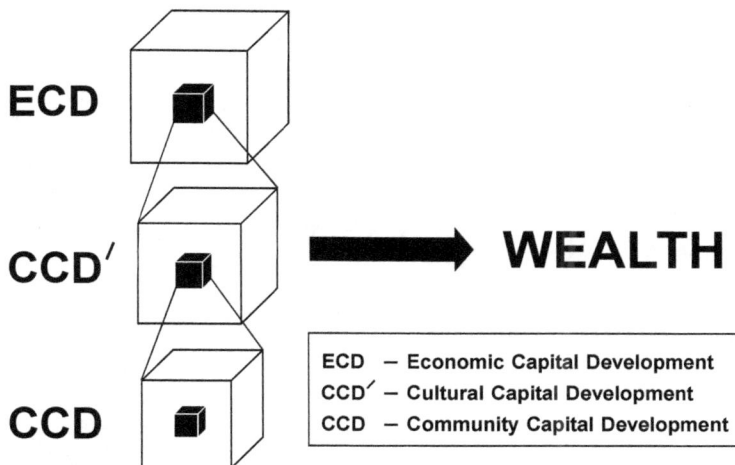

ECD

CCD′ ⟶ **WEALTH**

CCD

ECD	— Economic Capital Development
CCD′	— Cultural Capital Development
CCD	— Community Capital Development

Figure 24. The New Economic Paradigm

Community Capital Development

The Generativity Culture is built on the foundation of the Generative Community (see Figure 25). As may be noted, Community Capital Development (CCD) is developmentally and cumulatively the function of the components of the Generative Community. Just as we experienced culture shock nationally, so do communities experience culture shock locally. For example, while Springfield achieved the mission of the Generative Community in the 1970s and 1980s, it suffered the shock of losing its cultural "cellular bonding tissue" in the 1990s and 2000s.

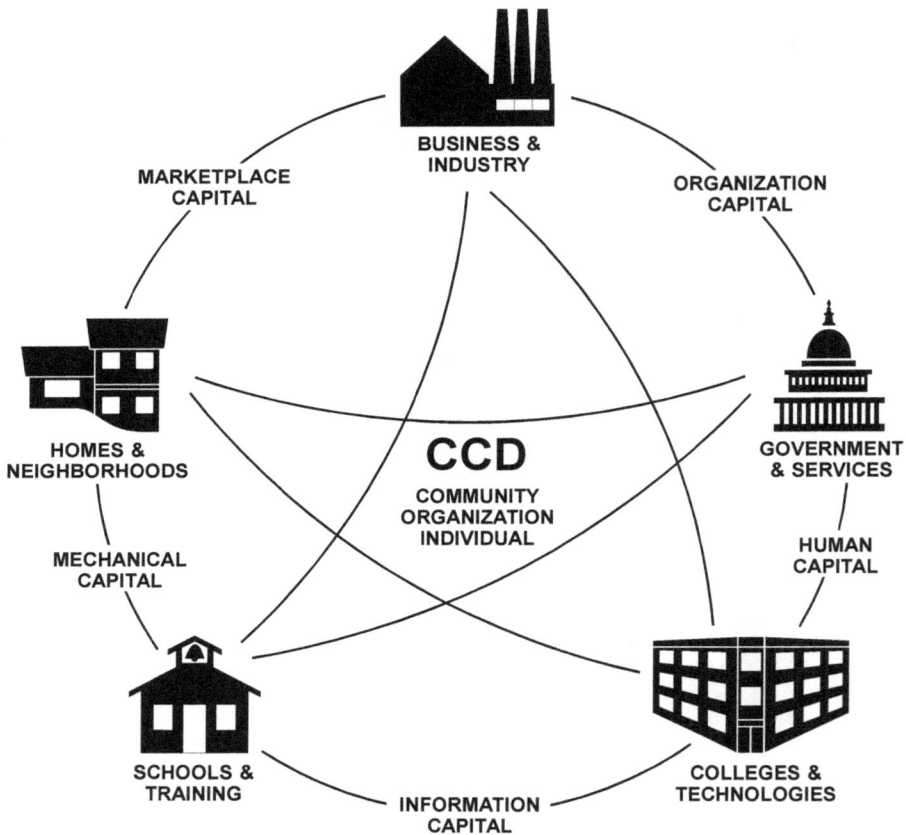

Figure 25. Community Capital Development (CCD)

Cultural Capital Development

Just as the community is a network of organizations within which networks of people function, so is the culture a network of communities (see Figure 26). These cultures are enduring communities that are held together by shared values. In the cases of cultures, the successful cultures around the world share the freedom functions. For example, while American culture was on the verge of fulfilling the freedom functions in 2000, it went into free-fall with the introduction of Totalitarian Socialism over the past decade.

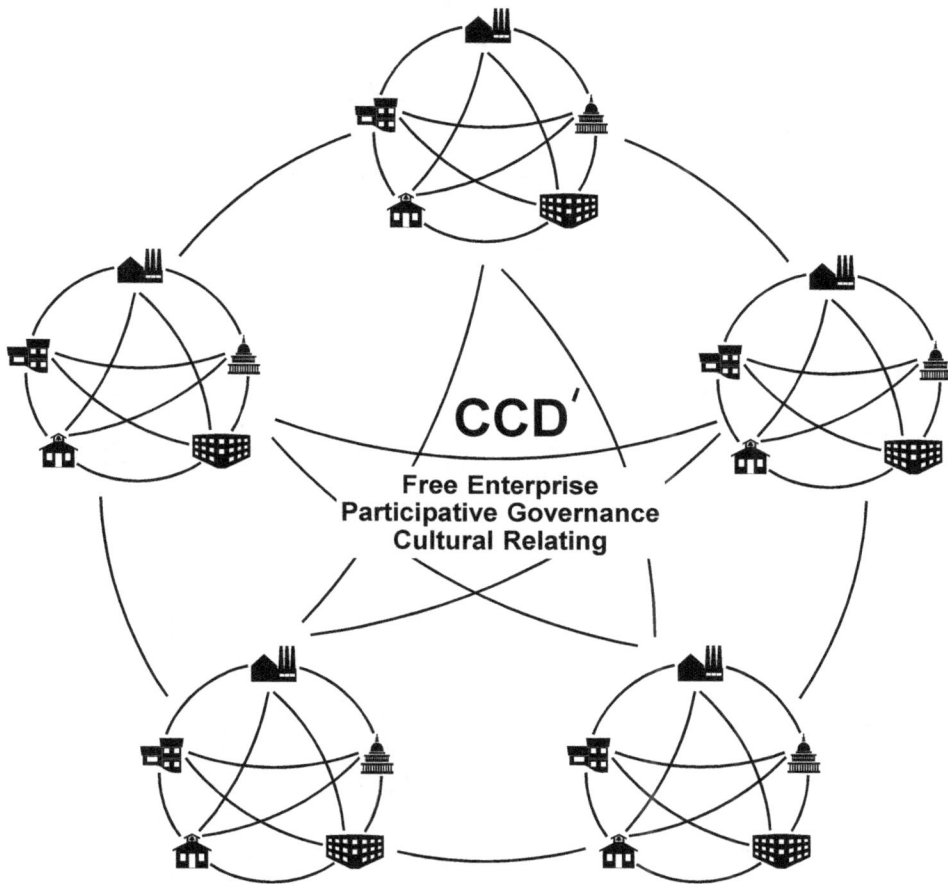

Figure 26. Cultural Capital Development

Economic Capital Development

The culminating image of socioeconomic growth is that of Economic Generativity (see Figure 27). Just as culture comprises networks of communities, so do economies comprise of networks of cultures that share a common vision or mission. For example, while America's economic prosperity has stalled over the past few years, it now has the generativity positioning and processing systems to reignite its flight toward potentially infinite prosperity.

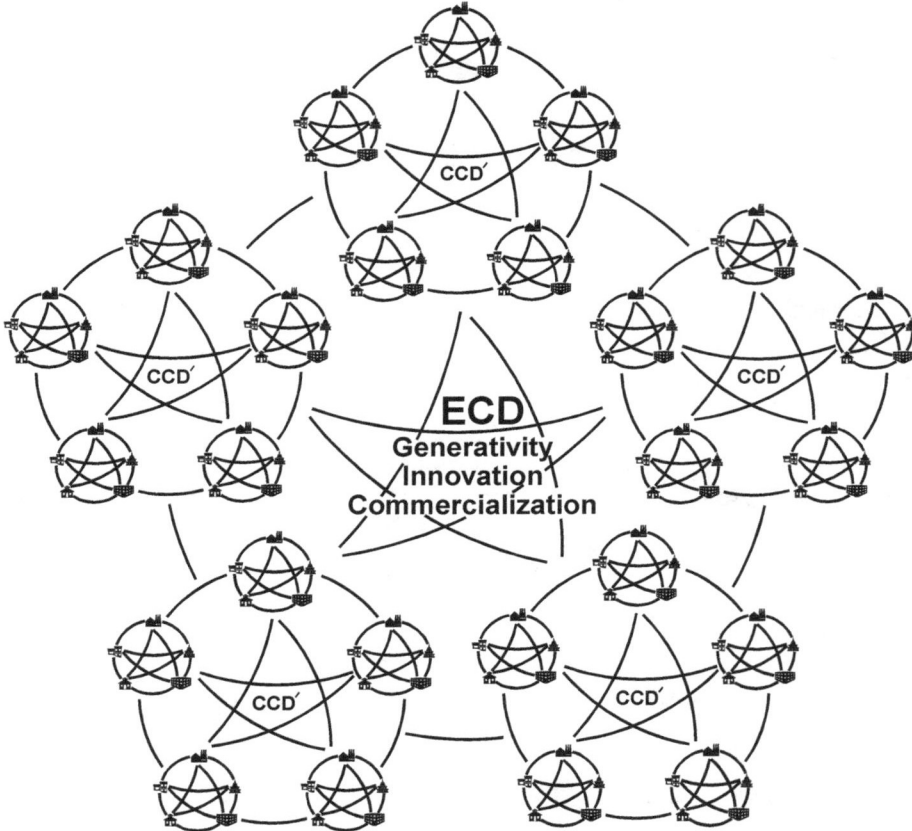

Figure 27. Economic Capital Development

High performances on our Economic Generativity Functions yield high returns in the "Pillars of Civilization:"

- **Generativity,** which generates breakthrough ideas

- **Innovation,** which innovates marketplace transfers

- **Commercialization,** which maximizes product values and profits

Together, these goals define the mission of Economic Capital Development or ECD.

The issues of supply-side and demand-side economics fade with the simultaneous courses of Economic Capital Development: We must build our new capital inductively through our communities (CCD) to our cultures (CCD′), even as we are generating our ideas and architectures deductively from our economic positioning (ECD).

In the final analysis, the recession of 2008–200? may be the best of all conditions for America, its citizens, and workers. The advanced capitalist nations will weather the financial crisis better than the less mature countries. This is because capitalism, itself, is "a theory of change": whatever ingredients are most important to our prosperity are incorporated into the wealth-generating equation.

Having lost their way, Americans now have the opportunity to re-examine their values and define the requirements to accomplish these values. Are we consumers or producers? Can we return again to the generativity that made us great? Are we still worthy of the leadership role?

The generative direction is the new capital ingredient in the economic equation. We can create our way out of any hole, no matter how deep. Moreover, we can generate a great new economy of abundance, where it is a privilege to live, learn, and, above all, work.

The overriding economic question is this: are we going to assume the economic conditions of stasis that have overtaken us over the last few decades? If so, then teach your children Mandarin and prepare them for a second-class commoditized consumer existence!

Or are we going to dedicate ourselves to the economic conditions of change—continuous change—where we generate the very conditions within which we operate? If so, then teach your children American and prepare them for a first-class generative producer existence!

In summary, Generativity is "The New Wealth of Nations."

Generativity is the path forward for Americans.

Hopefully, others will follow.

Chapter 9

"The Springfield Miracle"

In 1968, Dr. Richard C. Sprinthall initiated a program that came to be known as The Springfield Miracle.* Known as the "HRD Program," it was directed by Bob Carkhuff and Andrew H. Griffin. Funded by the CEOs of the two largest companies in town, Mass Mutual and Monarch Life, this program was soon to have profound effects upon all areas of the private and public sectors. Figure 27 at the end of this article will serve to guide the reader.

The Outcomes

The first issue is outcomes. Research principles of Applied Science dictate the measurement of outcomes by the effect of the intervening variable upon the dependent variable. So it is that an intervening variable such as HCD (Human Capital Development) intervenes upon the existing measures of socioeconomic functioning in Springfield: the effects upon human, information, organization, marketplace, community, cultural, and economic functions. In short, the intervention becomes the cause and the impact becomes the effect.

The Interventions

The second issue is interventions. Research principles of Applied Science also dictate the principles of intervention:

- The initiatives must be operational as they were in the physical, emotional, and intellectual skills-building programs of the HRD Center.

- The initiatives must be measurable as they were in the living, learning, and working functions of the HRD Center.

- The initiatives must be replicable as they were in the individual, interpersonal, and interdependent processes of the HRD Center.

In short, the intervention becomes the exemplary causes—components, functions, processes—for effecting powerful outcomes.

---

*Nocera, J. "The Springfield Miracle." *Newsweek,* June 6, 1988, pp. 45–48.

The Effects of Interventions on Outcomes

Each participating party in the Springfield HCD intervention viewed the outcomes in terms of their unique benefits. Thus, for example, the insurance corporations viewed the effects upon their presenting problem as cost-avoidance savings. In turn, the targeted marginal community of "The Hill" was viewed by the corporations as the source of their problems.

Corporate Benefits

The corporate benefits for Mass Mutual and Monarch Life insurance companies fell into two categories:

- **Cost-Avoidance Outcomes**

    - The companies avoided tens of billions of dollars by not having to move their headquarters from Springfield to other settings.

    - The companies avoided the millions of dollars in expenditures for reducing crises by expanding protection from employees.

    - The companies avoided the millions of dollars in expenditures for improving community relations by elevating corporate–community public relations.

- **Productivity Outcomes**

    - The companies improved the standards of individual employee performance by recruiting trained (**PTS—Productive Thinking Skills**) employees with specific skill competencies.

    - The companies improved the standards of unit productivity by incorporating interpersonally-skilled (**IPS—Interpersonal Processing Skills**) employees with specific skill competencies.

    - The companies improved the standards of organizational profitability by incorporating organizationally-skilled (**OPS—Organizational Processing Skills**) employees with specific skill competencies.

Community Benefits

The community benefits for citizens of "The Hill" and areas surrounding the insurance corporations emphasized personal and immediate benefits:

- **Education and Skills**
  Community members with an average seventh grade education received payment for one year of full-time college study (55% went on to complete college).

- **Employment and Salaries**
  Community members were employed in newly created positions in both the private and public sectors which removed them from the ranks of the unemployed and entered them as gainfully employed where, over 13 years, they out-earned the majority population.

- **Health and Citizenship**
  Community members converted to healthy practices for both themselves and their families (zero percent recidivated on crime), thus becoming constructive citizens in every respect.

College Benefits

The college benefits for acting as facilitator and expediter of logistics and other resources were direct and powerful:

- **Payments by Sponsors**
  Direct payments were made by the sponsoring insurance companies to compensate the college for its logistical and personnel support.

- **Publicity by Media**
  Publicity by all the media on all the processes and outcomes of intervention centered on the initiatives of the HRD Center and established A.I.C.'s reputation that it was working on real issues in the 1960s.

- **Applications for Enrollment**
  Directly related to publicity, applications for enrollment were increased by 15% or above, reflecting parental interest in college support for HRD initiatives (at a time when applications to all colleges in New England decreased).

City Benefits

The city of Springfield was receptive to all benefits received city-wide:

- The HRD Center provided leadership to all parties in making a transition from The Industrial Age City of Homes.

- The HRD Center provided leadership to all parties in introducing them to the early stages of The Information Age City of Communities.

- The HRD Center provided leadership to all parties in introducing them to conceptualization in processing the actuarial data of insurance business as well as the leaders of all other private and public sector organizations.

Culture Benefits

By attracting more than 10% of the general population, the HRD Center was generator of a series of movements that contributed to the elevation of culture—both nationally and internationally.

- The HRD Center generated the Human Technology Movement based upon the human and information skills-building programs it originated and disseminated.

- The HRD Center generated the Human Relations Movement based upon the Human Relations Skills-Building Technologies it originated and disseminated.

- The HRD Center generated the first phases of the Human Resource Development Movement based upon the HRD Model for Skills-Building in the Living, Learning, and Working functions it originated and disseminated.

The Issues of Outcome

Simply summarized, the issues of outcome are prepotent: powerful crises require powerful interventions that yield powerful benefits.

Our socioeconomic crises are powerful. We cannot transform them without powerful interventions such as HCD.

Our powerful interventions must transform all forms of NCD or New Capital Development as did HCD:

$$\textbf{HCD} \rightarrow \textbf{NCD}$$

Our powerful benefits will transform all forms of human endeavors by relating them interdependently (see Figure 27).

In transition, the issues of outcome are the issues of human growth and development:

> **Either we relate or
> we deteriorate!**

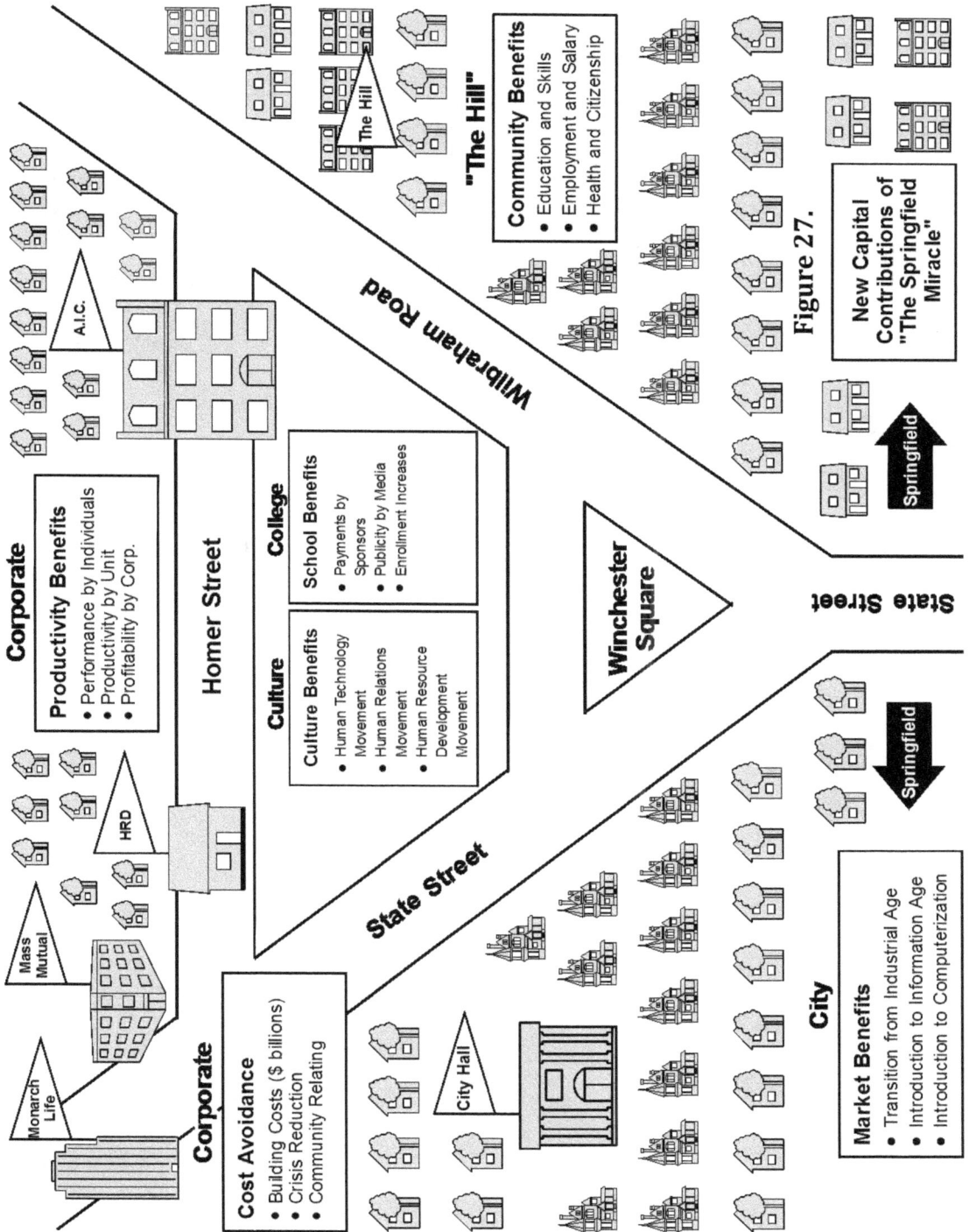

Figure 27.

"The Hill"

Community Benefits
- Education and Skills
- Employment and Salary
- Health and Citizenship

New Capital Contributions of "The Springfield Miracle"

Springfield

Corporate

Productivity Benefits
- Performance by Individuals
- Productivity by Unit
- Profitability by Corp.

Culture   **College**

Culture Benefits
- Human Technology Movement
- Human Relations Movement
- Human Resource Development Movement

School Benefits
- Payments by Sponsors
- Publicity by Media
- Enrollment Increases

Winchester Square

Homer Street

Wilbraham Road

State Street

State Street

Corporate

Cost Avoidance
- Building Costs ($ billions)
- Crisis Reduction
- Community Relating

City

Market Benefits
- Transition from Industrial Age
- Introduction to Information Age
- Introduction to Computerization

Springfield

A.I.C.

HRD

Mass Mutual

Monarch Life

City Hall

The Hill

Chapter 10

Freedom and Generativity

All freedoms begin with individual freedom. All individual freedom begins with thinking culminating in initiative. The following is an autobiographical history beginning with individual freedom leading to all forms of freedom—organizational, community, cultural, marketplace.

Andrew H. Griffin, Jr. was a poor black boy, born in the inner city of Springfield, Massachusetts, the sixth oldest of seventeen children. His father worked two jobs to support his family, and his mother spent long days providing the physical and psychological nourishment to a family that now includes more than 70 grandchildren. Andy, as he is now known to his professional colleagues, will always be "Bootsie" to the family from whom he has both drawn and given responsive strength and initiative support. Here is how he sees the development of his maturity.

Individual Freedom

I come from a family of seventeen and never thought of being poor until I went to college and they talked about poverty levels according to income and number of people in a family. I was taught to believe that no one was better than I, nor I better than anyone else. My parents taught us to recognize opportunity and that everyone should be given the same opportunity. They encouraged us to be individuals but demanded that we do our best, as well as be able to accept the consequences for whatever we did. My mother tended to be understanding. My father tended to be demanding. They complemented each other. Both my mother and father were very, very strong and had a 360-degree reinforcement program in all the areas. They loved and fought violently. It was an "either-or" world. You did or you didn't. It was very easy for me to understand that. They accepted all people, regardless of race, and allowed us to join or participate in all constructive activities. My sisters could play baseball and basketball equal to my brothers and myself. The idea of sexism was foreign to me. Although I recognized the difference in color, it was really the capabilities of a person that made a real difference.

As I grew up, my mother and father sat "upon my shoulders" *many times when I was about to make a major decision. More often than not, my behavior was influenced by what I thought they would have done. It is still from this background I draw much of my thinking, regardless of what the research or renowned people say. My early experiences in life with my mother and father provided me with the foundation for later life. Whatever I did, whether I felt comfortable or not, they were concerned that I did it with the best of my energies. Because my mother was able to remain at home, I knew that I was able to reach her at any time. Psychologically and realistically this provided me with a genuine support system. My father constantly assessed and challenged me in all the activities that I became a part of, including leading demonstrations that he did not fully appreciate.*

I also learned a lot of life's lessons in playing ball. Most of all, I learned not to place limits on my performance. I found I could do a lot of things that I did not think possible. I learned to do things better and better. I transferred these learnings to the classroom and learned to achieve in school.

*The first set of freedom-building skills that I learned was **individual thinking:***

- ***Exploring** by analyzing my experience*
- ***Understanding** by synthesizing my objectives*
- ***Acting** by operationalizing my programs*

*These skills empowered me to generate individual initiatives and, thus, my own **individual freedom.** I was ready to dedicate my individual thinking to larger purposes.*

Organizational Freedom

I always knew that there was a limit to what individuals could accomplish by themselves. I was oriented to participating, contributing, and finally leading in organizations. I viewed organizations like the teams that I played on:

- *The military, where I rose to sergeant in the U.S. Marines*

- *Football, where I rose to the professional level with the Green Bay Packers*

- *College, where I rose to the doctoral level with a Harvard degree*

- *Education, where I rose to Assistant Superintendent of Education in the state of Washington, leading educator in the union*

*However, what really facilitated the explosion of my growth was participating as co-director and then director of the Center for Human Resource Development at a small college, American International College, in the middle of a black ghetto. This organization was dedicated to the mission of Human Resource Development, or HRD. The second set of **freedom-building** skills that I learned was **organizational processing systems.** We all worked interdependently to develop all organizational functions:*

- *Policy-making for positioning ourselves to relate to people and human resources*

- *Executive architecture to develop skills programs and curricula to empower people*

- *Management systems to manage skills development programs for community people, undergraduates, and graduate students*

- *Supervisory processes to achieve skills objectives in all areas of HRD*

- *Delivery programs to implement the tasks to achieve the HRD objectives*

Above all else, I learned to think—individually and interpersonally:

- *Getting others' images of things*
- *Giving my images of things*
- *Merging our mutual images of things*

*With this backdrop, I adopted the theme: **"Ain't no stoppin' us now!"***

*Our organizational units were focused interdependently: **"Mutual processing for mutual objectives."***

Community

*We emphasized the community as a **"network of organizations."** These skills empowered us to generate organizational initiatives and, thus, achieve our **organizational freedom.***
We focused upon the community by viewing all other entities in the community:

- *Homes, neighborhoods and churches*
- *Schools and training programs*
- *Higher education and technology*
- *Government and its services*
- *Business and industry*

*The third set of **freedom-building** skills that I learned was **community processing systems:** We related to all of these entities interdependently.*

- *To develop parenting and early childhood programs as well as **Head-Start** programs for basic **"learning-to-learn"** needs*

- *To develop educational and tutorial programs to accelerate the development of skills in conventional education systems and **new careers** programs for people with nonconventional needs*

- *To develop higher education and technologies for advanced training programs in higher-order generative processing systems*

- *To elevate governance and service programs in the basic needs of housing, welfare, justice and recreation systems*

- *To elevate business and industry's community involvement by engaging them in enlightened policy-making with community leaders while supplying them with improved human capital for their work requirements*

In short, we assumed leadership in initiating and coordinating programs "from womb to tomb." These skills empowered us to generate community initiatives and, thus, achieve our Community Freedom.

Culture

*Most of my life, I thought of community as the highest order of organization. As I mentioned, I understood that culture itself was no more—nor less—than a **"network of communities"** and what they believe about themselves.*
I began working with different cultures in what we labeled ethnic think tanks:

- *Black cultures*
- *White cultures*
- *Hispanic cultures*
- *Asian cultures*
- *Island cultures*

Each of these cultures conceived of themselves in terms of their uniqueness. Each discovered their commonalities: They were indeed "communities of communities."

In this context, I discovered my fourth set of freedom-building skills to be cultural processing systems:

- *"How did the cultures want to relate to other cultures?"*
- *"How would they support these relationships economically?"*
- *"How would they support these relationships governmentally?"*

The answers we discovered were truly rational.

Most everyone wanted to relate independently with other cultures (without understanding that relating and independence constitute an oxymoron or a conflict in meaning).

Most everyone realized that they need to commit to some form or another of capitalistic economics in order to accomplish this independence.

Most everyone recognized that they required supportive representative governance to implement the capitalism and accomplish the independence mission.

With each cultural grouping, we were able to summarize the functions to which free cultures aspire:

- *Cultural relating*
- *Free enterprise economics*
- *Free and direct democratic governance*

*We label these the **freedom functions.** We dedicate our cultures to achieving them. These skills empowered us to generate cultural initiatives and, thus, achieve our **cultural freedom.***

Marketplace

*It has been in my maturity that I began to understand the role of cultures in defining the marketplace: **"The marketplace is a network of cultures."** My fifth set of **freedom-building** skills was **marketplace processing systems.***

I began working with different cultures to define the marketplace for their contributions. Working with the leaders of each culture, we established training cadres for exporting our learnings and skills to other cultures.

*Again, in meeting with other cultures, we defined each other in terms of the **freedom functions.** Most often, we found that these newly addressed cultures were functioning at low levels:*

- *Dependent cultural relating*
- *Controlled economics*
- *Totalitarian governance*

*We worked with them to elevate both their perspectives and their performance on the **freedom functions.** These skills empowered us to generate marketplace initiatives and, thus, achieve our **marketplace freedom.***

Together, the skills programs that we designed ran parallel to the experiences that I have detailed:

- *Individual initiative leading to **individual freedom***
- *Organizational initiative leading to **organizational freedom***

- *Community initiative leading to **community freedom***
- *Cultural initiative leading to **cultural freedom***
- *Marketplace initiative leading to **marketplace freedom***

In all instances, we empowered the cultures in the skills that they required to participate in "The Global Village and Its Marketplace."

*We labeled the freedom-building projects, **The Seed of Freedom,** and deliver them to you now. It all begins with individual freedom.*

Before initiating Freedom-Building Programs, we must refer to the models we are employing.

The Freedom Model may be viewed in its totality in Figure 28. As may be noted, the freedom functions are accomplished by **New Capital Development** or **NCD Components** enabled by **Generative Thinking Processes** or **The New 3Rs Processes:**

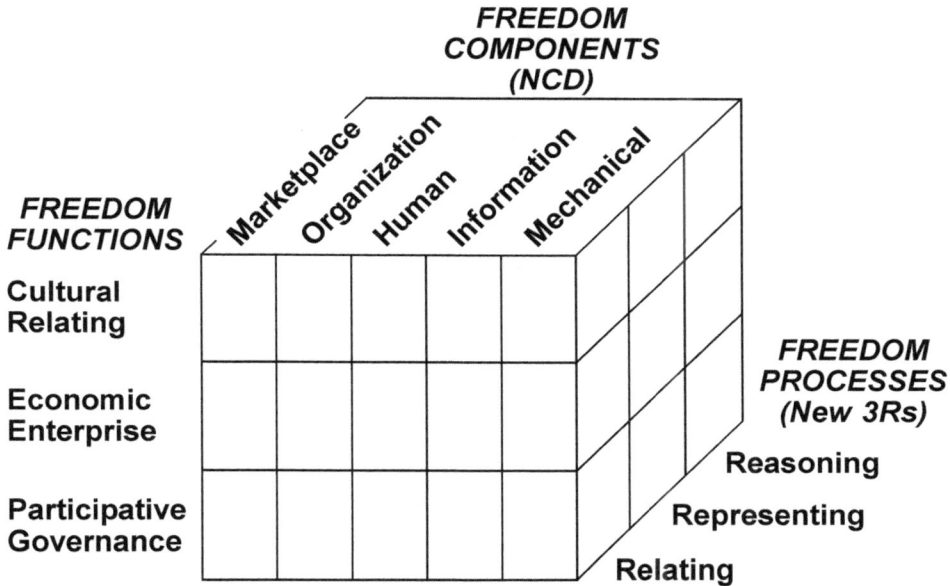

Figure 28. The Freedom Model

This means that we accomplish our freedom functions by new capital development enabled by Generative Thinking Systems. In short, we need to think initiatively in order to participate entrepreneurially in accomplishing the freedom functions.

In short, there is a Model for Initiating in the Global Marketplace—to participate, to contribute, to lead. It remains for us to make intentional and, indeed, initiative decisions to do so. What follow are the empowerment programs for individual, organizational, community, cultural, and marketplace initiatives for achieving freedom.

Phase I—Empowering Individual Initiatives

Goal: To empower individual initiative by training in the **New 3Rs of Thinking Skills** (see Figure 29).

Objectives: **The New 3Rs of Thinking**

- **R¹—Relating skills** that enable individuals to relate productively by getting, giving, and merging information

- **R²—Representing skills** that enable individuals to represent information productively in sentences, systems and scales

- **R³—Reasoning skills** that enable individuals to reason with information powerfully by exploring, understanding, and acting initiatively upon the information

Benefits: **New 3Rs → Individual Initiatives**

- **Living functions** such as home and family

- **Learning functions** such as education and training

- **Working functions** such as performance and production

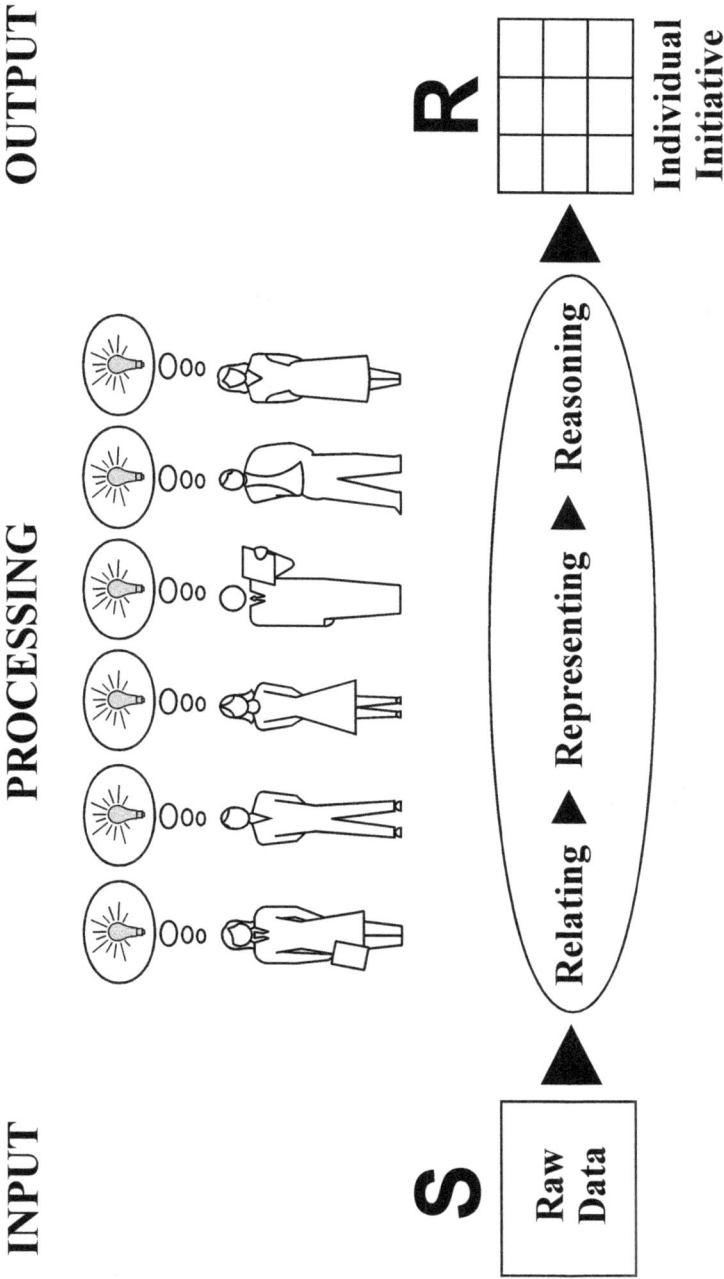

Figure 29. Empowering Individual Freedom

Phase II—Empowering Organizational Initiatives

Goal: To empower organizations to make community initiatives "**I**" by acquiring and applying the **New Capital Development Systems** (see Figure 30).

Objectives: **The New Capital Development Systems**

- **MCD—marketplace capital development** or positioning in the marketplace

- **OCD—organizational capital development** or aligning organization resources with positioning

- **HCD—human capital development** or human processing to implement organization alignment

- **ICD—information capital development** or information modeling to implement human processing

- **mCD—mechanical capital development** or mechanical tooling to implement information modeling

Benefits: **New 3Rs x NCD → Organizational Initiatives**

- **Policy functions** such as missioning

- **Executive functions** such as organizing

- **Management functions** such as systematizing

- **Supervisory functions** such as operationalizing

- **Delivery functions** such as technologizing

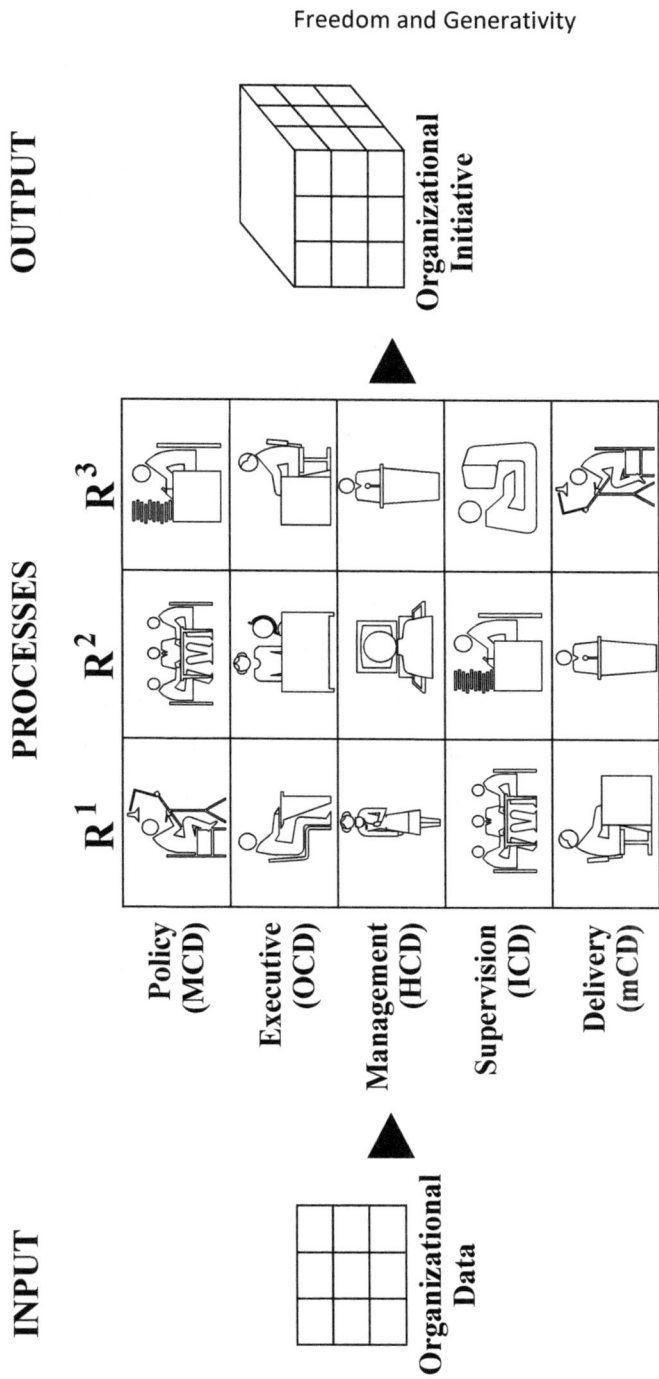

Figure 30. Empowering Organizational Freedom

Phase III—Empowering Community Initiatives

Goal: To empower organizations to make community initiatives **"I"** by acquiring and applying the **New Capital Development Systems** (see Figure 31).

Objectives: **Community Capital Development Systems**

- Homes and Neighborhoods emphasizing **mCD**
- Education and Training emphasizing **mCD** and **ICD**
- Higher Education emphasizing **mCD, ICD,** and **HCD**
- Governance emphasizing **mCD, ICD, HCD,** and **OCD**
- Business emphasizing **mCD, ICD, HCD, OCD,** and **MCD**

Benefits: **New 3Rs x NCD → Community Initiatives**

- **Home functions** to prepare people to relate to information
- **School functions** to empower learners to represent information
- **College functions** to empower thinkers to reason with information
- **Governance functions** to empower organizations to process community information and align resources
- **Business functions** to empower corporations to process marketing information and position community

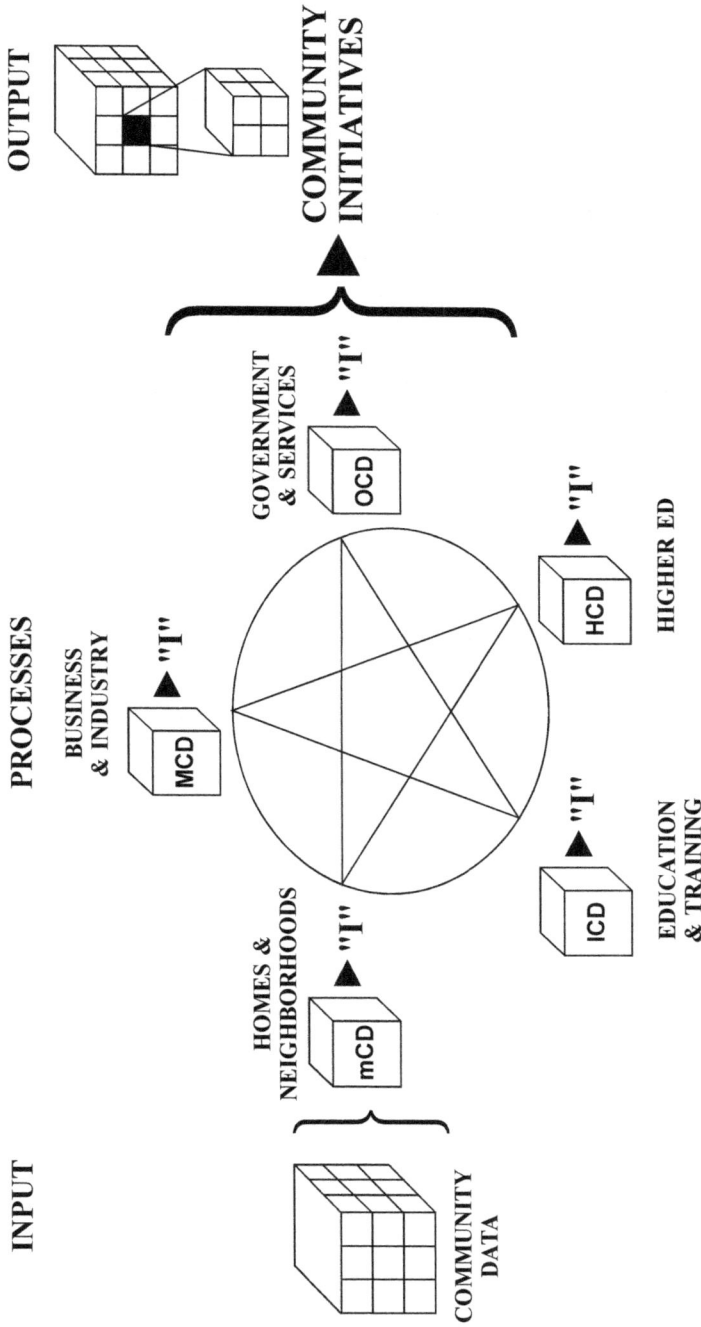

Figure 31. Empowering Community Freedom

Phase IV—Empowering Cultural Initiatives

Goal: To empower communities to make cultural initiatives by acquiring and applying the **Freedom Functions** (see Figure 32).

Objectives: **The Freedom Functions (FF)**

- **Cultural relating** to initiate collaboratively with other communities
- **Free enterprise** to initiate entrepreneurially in economics with other communities
- **Participative governance** to initiate directly in governance with other communities

Benefits: **New 3Rs x NCD x Freedom Functions (FF) → Cultural Initiatives**

- **Initiative thinking** in individuals
- **Individual integration** in organizations
- **Organizational integration** in communities
- **Community integration** in cultures
- **Cultural integration** in marketplace

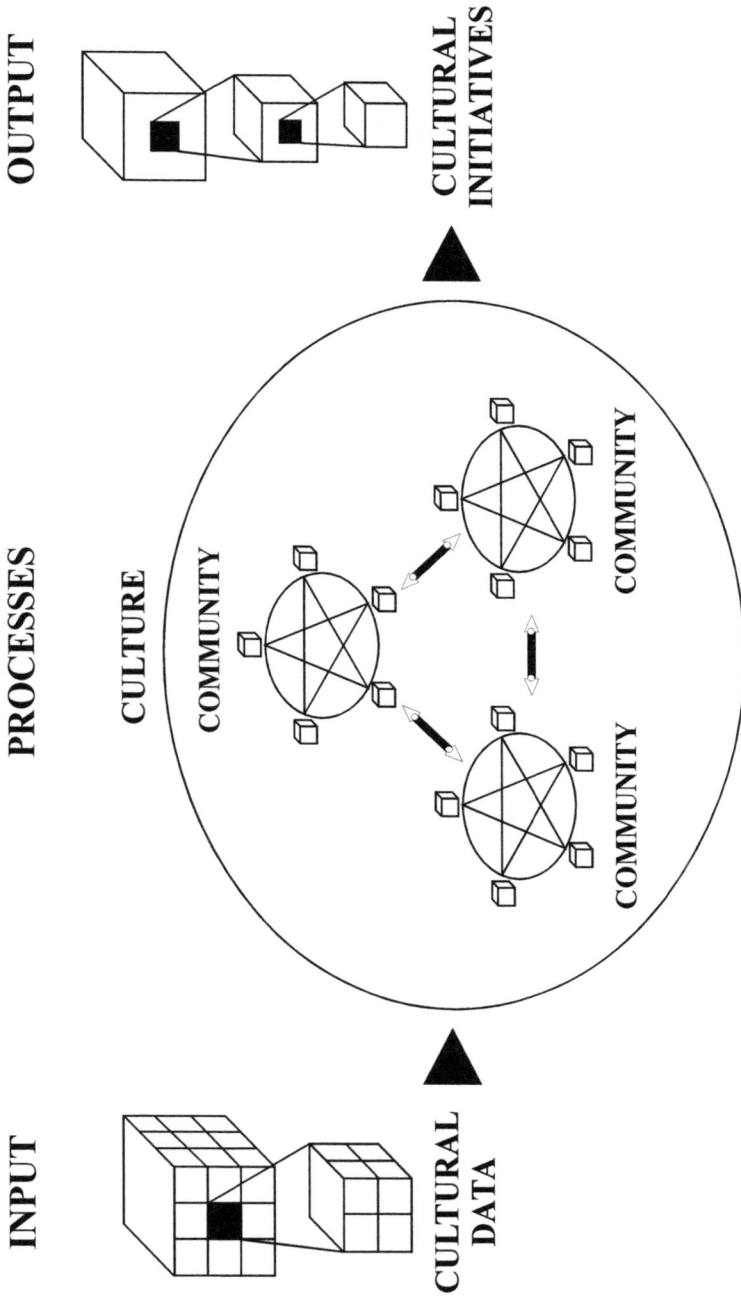

Figure 32. Empowering Cultural Freedom

Phase V—Empowering Marketplace Initiatives

Goal: To empower cultures to make marketplace initiatives by acquiring and applying the **Freedom Doctrine Design** (see Figure 33).

Objectives: **The Freedom Doctrine Systems**

- Freedom Functions (FF)
- New Capital Development (NCD) Components
- The New 3Rs Processes

Benefits: **Freedom Doctrine → Marketplace Initiatives**

- New 3Rs → Individual Initiative
- New 3Rs x NCD → Organizational Initiative
- New 3Rs x NCD → Community Initiative
- New 3Rs x NCD x FF → Cultural Initiative
- Freedom Doctrine → Marketplace Initiative

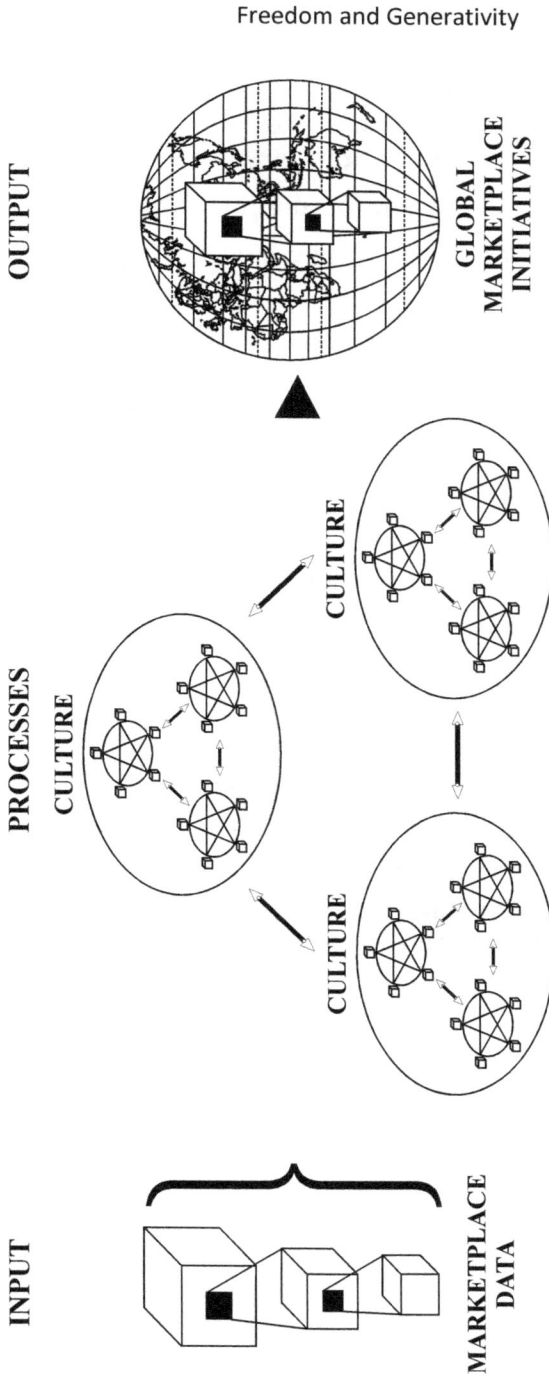

Figure 33. Empowering Marketplace Freedom

In summary, the mission of freedom-building may be viewed in the Freedom Model (see again Figure 33): To develop the **Architecture for Global Freedom.** This architecture culminates in the **Global Village and Its Marketplace:**

I.   Empowering individual initiatives by training in the New 3Rs Thinking Skills

II.   Empowering organizational initiatives by dedicating the New 3Rs to organizational functions

III. Empowering community initiatives by training in the New Capital Development Systems

IV.   Empowering cultural initiatives by training in the Freedom Functions

V.   Empowering marketplace initiatives by relating the Cultural Systems

The marketplace initiatives culminate in the first model for the Global Village and Its Marketplace. Indeed, the freedom-building websites will provide the first demonstrable and measurable indices of the existence of the Global Village and Its Marketplace.

In summary, the facts of its existence are worth reviewing:

- The Internet and other Information Age phenomena have created a Global Village and Its Marketplace.

- The Global Marketplace has shifted the source of socioeconomic growth to human brainpower and the NCD that it generates in the New Age of Ideation.

- Our human brainpower has shifted the emphasis to human processing as the source of initiative—intrapreneurial, entrepreneurial, extrapreneurial.

In transition, it is the very individualism that has characterized the American experience that the world needs to emulate and—dare we say—imitate. For we are now made in the image of a global village.

Individualism and global freedom! One is not possible without the other!

Chapter 11

The Generativity Civilization

Along with researchers at the Heritage Foundation, our intentions have been to measure the degrees of socioeconomic freedoms and relate them to the levels of economic prosperity.

The economic freedoms are defined as follows:

> ...all liberties and rights of production, distribution, or consumption of goods and services.

A sample of the corollaries of economic freedoms follow:

- Absolute rights of property ownership and constitutional law
- Fully realized movements for labor, capital, and goods
- Absolute absences of coercions or constraints of economic liberty

In short, individual entrepreneurs would be free to produce and consume in any way under the rule of law. Moreover, their freedom would be at once protected and respected by the state.

While the necessity for governmental intervention for the "public good" is stipulated, governmental coercion that rises above the minimal level is considered "corrosive to freedom"—most notably economic freedom.

The 10 specific economic freedoms measured in the 2009 Index of Economic Freedom are identified below. Each of the freedoms is individually scored. A country's overall economic freedom score is an average of its scores on the 10 individual freedoms:

- Business freedom
- Trade freedom
- Fiscal freedom
- Government size
- Monetary freedom
- Investment freedom
- Financial freedom
- Property rights
- Corruption freedom
- Labor freedom

In perspective, the 10 factors emphasize governmental activities that facilitate or retard free economic enterprise. They are not, themselves, indices of the governance processes for generating initiatives that enhance or constrain free enterprise. To obtain these indices, we must study the nature of governance processes, ranging from totalitarian to free democratic. Nor are these 10 factors indices of economic performance. To obtain performance indices, we must study the relationships of these broad factors with individual or per capita GDP.

The sources of economic growth and prosperity may be summarized globally with data on economic freedom and per capita GDP (see Figure 34). The correlation relating "Economic Freedom Scores" to GDP indices is +0.69. This means that we can account for approximately 50% of the variance in economic prosperity and growth by a country's level of free enterprise:

- Those countries that engage in free enterprise are economically prosperous and growthful.

- Those countries that emphasize command-and-control economies are economically poor and stagnant.

In summary, economic prosperity is highly related to economic freedoms.

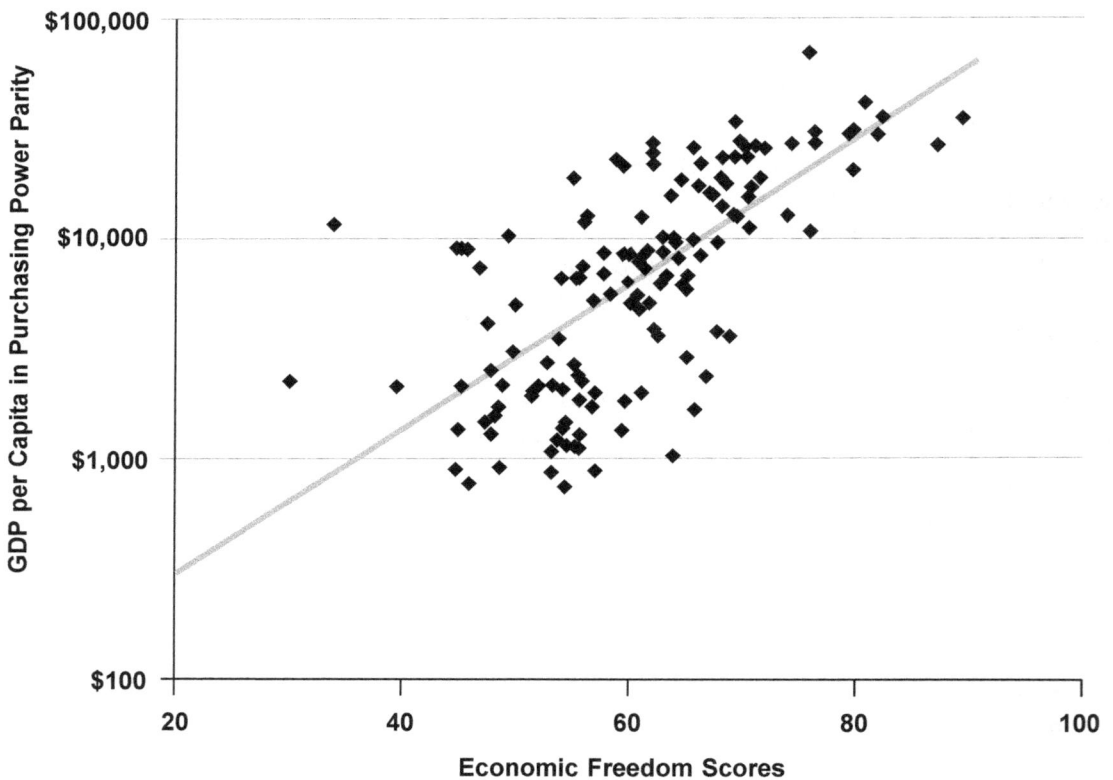

**Figure 34. Free Enterprise and Per Capita Income
(2009 Index of Economic Freedom)**

It is important to emphasize that both the absolute levels and the changes in levels of economic freedom scores are predictors of economic growth and prosperity. Those countries that increased economic freedom grew more than a percentage point faster than those countries that lost economic freedom, averaging an annual growth rate of 3.3% in per capita GDP versus the laggard's average of 1.9%.

Emphatically, over the 15-year period of assessment, those countries that gained more than 5 points of economic freedom reduced poverty over 5.8% while those countries that lost more than 5 points of economic freedom lost an additional 0.4% of their people to poverty.

It is noteworthy that the economic freedom scores also relate highly with other important human benefits:

- Indices of democracy are correlated at +0.67, accounting for 45% of democratic governance.

- Indices of human development are correlated at +0.63, accounting for 40% of overall quality of life.

- Indices of environmental development are correlated at +0.55, accounting for 30% of environmental sustainability.

All of this is part of a database that we have replicated and trust. A sustained commitment to economic freedom fosters human and environmental development as well as prosperity and equity of distribution.

Generative Entrepreneurs

President Obama has characterized small, entrepreneurial-type businesses as "ma-and-pa" operations in his mind, grossing no more than $250,000 per year. Indeed, many of the people he met on the streets of Chicago fit this description. However well this characterization may work for taxation or regulation, or even voter registration, it flat-out misses the critical contributions of entrepreneurial enterprise to the American economy. Moreover, how on earth does he reconcile this immature image of small, entrepreneurial businesses with their prepotent contributions to the economy? Under conditions of economic freedom:

- Entrepreneurial enterprise generates as much as 80% of the scientific breakthroughs and technological innovations.

- Entrepreneurial enterprise generates as much as 80% of the new jobs in implementing the follow-throughs on the technological innovations.

- Entrepreneurial enterprise generates as much as 50% of America's GDP.

To be sure, an overwhelming case can be made for the prepotency of entrepreneurial enterprise over all other sources of economic growth:

- Entrepreneurial enterprise dwarfs the contributions of all governmental sources, including the presidency, congress, and the federal sector that they manage.

Yet these entrepreneurial businesses are exploited by the multinational corporations of the private sector who, like Bill Gates of Microsoft, track them and trap them if they have attractive commercial products or services, "making them offers they can't refuse."

Moreover, they are passed over by the bureaucratic czars of the public sector who favor "sole-source contracts" with "soul-less contacts," while simultaneously taxing and regulating American entrepreneurs out of existence in the fabled American "meritocracy," "giving orders they can't follow."

To be sure, not all entrepreneurs are generative, capable of creating scientific "breakthroughs" and innovative technologies. By our estimates, no more than one in 100 entrepreneurs are currently generative; therefore somewhere around 50,000 people out of five million small businesses qualify as "generative entrepreneurs." In business, they may be labeled as "process engineers," capable of designing themselves and others out of their jobs. In government, they may be characterized as "social engineers," capable of defining spaces and empowering people to fill them.

The point is this: the other 99 of us live, learn, and work in the "draft" of their sciences, empowered by the tools of their technologies, prospering through their intelligence, their perspectives, and their good will.

In transition, America has had a unique form of capitalism, unlike any other nation. From the very founding of this country, entrepreneurs have been in the forefront. Indeed, we may say that entrepreneurs founded this country by overthrowing King George II. We may further say that these founding fathers and mothers—like John and Abigail Adams—defined this "Great Experiment" termed America.

To be sure, Adams, Franklin, and Jefferson continue to be the models for the term "entrē," or freedom of access. Even as he led the American armies, Washington fed the American armies. In the ultimate of risk-taking ventures, the outcome of the war dictated the terms of his life: if he won, he thrived; if he lost, he died.

The American economic engine has always been driven by her entrepreneurs. Great and small, they have shaped our socioeconomic progress. Known and unknown, they have generated the initiatives that brought us to where we are.

The great entrepreneurs of the 20th century come to mind: Edison (electricity), Ford (autos), Rockefeller (oil), and Morgan (finance) met regularly and shaped American policy.

Less known but more brilliant is the work of George Washington Carver. Driven by a mission to empower and free enslaved black peoples, he generated the sciences (biology), innovated the technologies (agrarian), developed the curricula (education), and distributed "best practices" (dissemination) to empower the most productive farmers in the Agrarian Age.

Webster defines entrepreneur as follows:

> The person who organizes, manages, and assumes the risks of a business; a successful businessman.

While our founding fathers were certainly defined by these characterizations, the conditions of our times have generated and, indeed, demand a new and more powerful set of requirements:

The person who generates an innovative idea, positions related products and services for comparative advantage in the marketplace, and capitalizes by organizing resources for productivity and profitability

As I sit here in the office of my expanding businesses, I wonder about the future of entrepreneurial enterprise. The data indicate that entrepreneurial enterprise is the driving engine of our economy. The data also indicate that entrepreneurial enterprise is the social ethic of our civilization. Finally, my experience suggests that there is a tangible set of learnable skills to prepare people for generative entrepreneurism.

The Conditions of Civilization

It is common in the Western world to identify the cradle of civilization as the Fertile Crescent, including especially Levant and Mesopotamia. Defining civilization as agrarian, urban, and culturally related, current thinkers have conjectured that there is no one cradle. Instead, they believe that several civilizations evolved independently, of which the Near Eastern Neolithic was the first to be identified. The enduring characterization of civilization has been the civilized way that cultures have related. This cultural relating factor applies to both homogeneous cultures such as Japan and heterogeneous cultures such as China and Asia. Other cultures have evolved through the ages reaching to open the Gordian Knot of civilization. While many have achieved hierarchical relating within cultures, few have demonstrated equitable relating between cultures, and none have attained judicious relating among cultures.

CULTURAL RELATING

The Core Conditions of Civilization

The Democracy Experiments—Greece

In the history of humankind, there have been three great movements toward freedom for civilization. Each constitutes a vital experiment in the representation of human experience and the realization of human potential. Together, they defined the foundation for the Western world. The first freedom movement was embodied in the democratic government of ancient Greece in Athens. Pericles demonstrated for the world that direct democratic participation was possible. Even though flawed by the limited size of the Athenian citizenry and the exclusion of the slaves on which it was built, this demonstration was nonetheless the initial step toward a new view of the relationship between people and government. While other nations attempted to follow this ideal, expressions of democracy were neutralized by the pathology of classism derived from narcissism and its instruments of servitude (Rome and England).

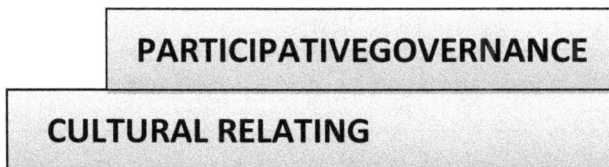

PARTICIPATIVEGOVERNANCE
CULTURAL RELATING

The Developmental Conditions of Democratic Civilization

The Free Enterprise Experiment—U.S.A.

The second great movement toward freedom was the American system, founded more than 200 years ago. Basing their ideas on the works of European philosophers such as Locke, Hobbes, and Hume, the Founding Fathers demonstrated that not only representative democratic governance was possible, but also that free enterprise economics was its driving engine. Of course, the American system was also flawed by withholding full freedoms and rights from first Americans, women, blacks, and other people of color. However, this flaw was not fatal. Our founders were politically conscious enough to give us an amending instrument to enact changes in the movement toward full freedom: the U.S. Constitution. The equality of all "men" having been declared, it remained for the disenfranchised to seek and achieve their own civil and human rights through amendments to the Constitution.

Indeed, today the U.S. stands alone as the beacon of democracy and free enterprise in the world:

- Its 50 states, some of them larger than most countries, relate peacefully and productively in the freest social system the world has ever known.

- Its 50 states, many of which would be among the most prosperous of countries, conduct the freest and most powerful wealth-generating economic systems in the history of the world.

- The citizens of its 50 states are constitutionally the policymakers of the freest representative democratic governance of the most powerful nation in the history of the world.

The U.S. has truly demonstrated itself to be the "Great Experiment." And it has been validated by all known measurements!

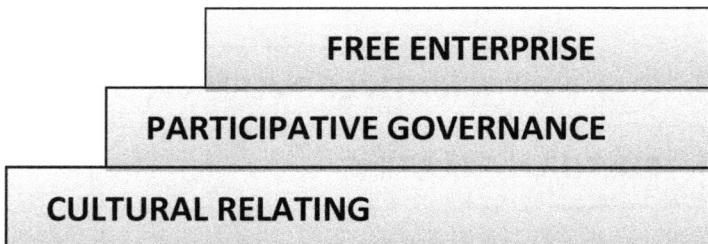

FREE ENTERPRISE

PARTICIPATIVE GOVERNANCE

CULTURAL RELATING

The Culminating Conditions of Free Enterprise Civilization

The New Capitalism Experiment—Global

Defining new capital as "what is most important," the third freedom movement has generated the greatest waves of prosperity in the history of humankind. Over the past 50 years, the new capitalism has out-generated the cumulative wealth of our entire history. To be sure, in the process, the new capitalism has made every individual, every community, every culture, every nation more prosperous than they were before 1960.

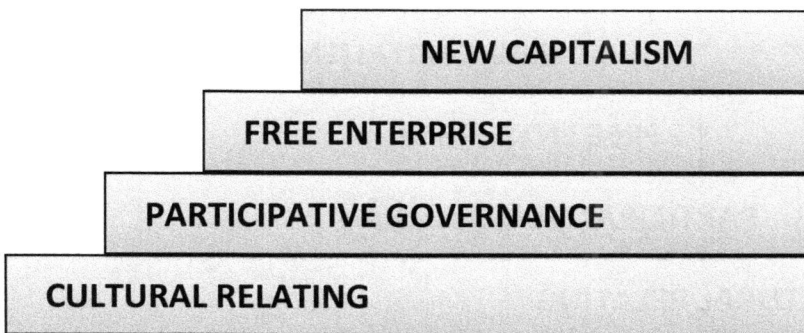

NEW CAPITALISM

FREE ENTERPRISE

PARTICIPATIVE GOVERNANCE

CULTURAL RELATING

The Cumulating Conditions of the New Capitalism

The Generativity Experiment

Evolving in our times, the potential for the fourth freedom movement is projected by the Generativity Doctrine, which offers a futuristic vision of the global village and its marketplace. Informed by the spiraling achievements of the American experiment, the Generativity Doctrine points civilization toward an elevated and integrated global society based on the fundamental proposition of Global Freedom: "All people are created equal in their potential for empowerment in generativity." The functions of such generativity incorporate the culminating conditions of generativity:

- Free and interdependent cultural relating
- Free and fully participative governance
- Entrepreneurially driven, free enterprise economics

The methods for achieving these freedom functions tell the story of the Generativity Doctrine.

We are thus called to engage in the Next Great Experiment—to build our people, our communities, all cultures, and all nations into an elevated, interdependent and, above all else, generative global society. This is the Generativity Doctrine. It will generate the Next Great Civilization! And it will be validated again and again!

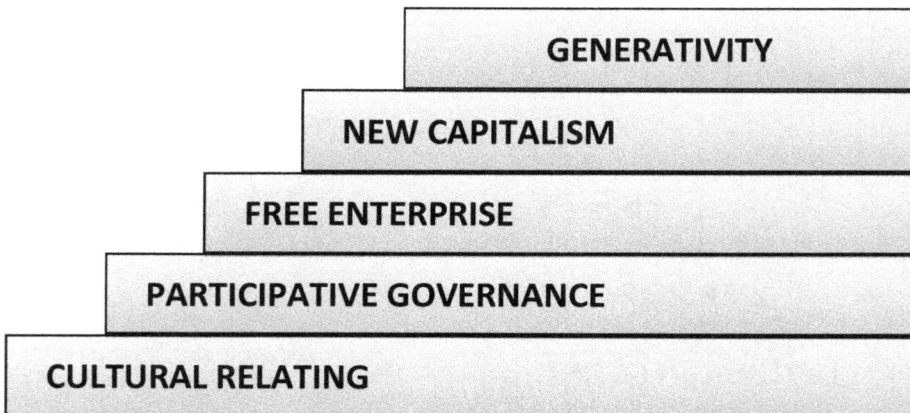

GENERATIVITY

NEW CAPITALISM

FREE ENTERPRISE

PARTICIPATIVE GOVERNANCE

CULTURAL RELATING

The Explosive Conditions of Generativity

References

- Human Sciences
- Information Sciences

Human Sciences

Anthony, W. *The Principles of Psychiatric Rehabilitation.* Baltimore, MD: University Park Press, 1979.

Aspy, D. N., and Roebuck, F. N. *Kids Don't Learn from People They Don't Like.* Amherst, MA: HRD Press, 1977.

Banks, G. *From Bondage through Prosperity: Finding the Freedom in Thinking.* Amherst, MA: HRD Press, 2013.

Berenson, B. G. *The Possibilities Mind.* Amherst, MA: HRD Press, 2001.

Berenson, B. G. *Carkhuff and The Human Sciences.* McLean, VA: The McLean Project, 2013.

Berenson, B. G. and Cannon, J. R. *The Science of Freedom.* Amherst, MA: HRD Press, 2006.

Berners-Lee, T. *Weaving the Web.* Britain: Orion Business, 1989, ISBN 0-7528-2090-7.

Bierman, R. *Toward Meeting Fundamental Human Service Needs.* Guelph, Ontario: Human Service Community, Inc., 1976.

Bugelski, B. R. *Psychology of Learning.* New York: Holt, Rinehart & Winston, 1956.

Bugelski, B. R. *Principles of Learning.* New York: Praeger, 1979.

Carkhuff, R. R. *Helping and Human Relations. Volumes 1 and II.* New York: Holt, Rinehart & Winston, 1969.

Carkhuff, R. R. *The Development of Human Resources.* New York: Holt, Rinehart & Winston, 1971.

Carkhuff, R. R. *The Promise of America.* Amherst, MA: HRD Press, 1974.

Carkhuff, R. R. *Toward Actualizing Human Potential.* Amherst, MA: HRD Press, 1981.

Carkhuff, R. R. *Sources of Human Productivity.* Amherst, MA: HRD Press, 1983.

Carkhuff, R. R. *The Exemplar.* Amherst, MA: HRD Press, 1984.

Carkhuff, R. R. *Human Processing and Human Productivity.* Amherst, MA: HRD Press, 1986.

Carkhuff, R. R. *The Age of the New Capitalism.* Amherst, MA: HRD Press, 1988.

Carkhuff, R. R. *Empowering.* Amherst, MA: HRD Press, 1989.

Carkhuff, R. R. *Human Possibilities.* Amherst, MA: HRD Press, 2000.

Carkhuff, R. R. *The Age of Ideation.* Amherst, MA: HRD Press, 2007.

Carkhuff, R. R. *The Art of Helping.* Ninth Edition. Amherst, MA: HRD Press, 2009.

Carkhuff, R. R. *Saving America: The Generativity Solution.* Amherst, MA: HRD Press, 2010.

Carkhuff, R.R. *The Human Sciences: Volume I. Probabilities, Possibilities, and Generativity Sciences.* Amherst, MA: HRD Press, 2013.

Carkhuff, R.R. *The Human Sciences: Volume II. Probabilities, Possibilities, and Generativity Technologies.* Amherst, MA: HRD Press, 2013.

Carkhuff, R. R. *TheMcLeanProject.com.* The McLean Project, 2011.

Carkhuff, R. R. *Human Generativity: An Introduction to Human Sciences.* Amherst, MA: HRD Press, 2013.

Carkhuff, R. R. and Berenson, B. G. *The New Science of Possibilities. Volumes I and II.* Amherst, MA: HRD Press, 2000.

Carkhuff, R. R. and Berenson, B. G., et al. *The Possibilities Organization.* Amherst, MA: HRD Press, 2000.

Carkhuff, R. R. and Berenson, B. G., et al. *The Possibilities Leader.* Amherst, MA: HRD Press, 2000.

Carkhuff, R. R. and Berenson, B. G., et al. *The Freedom Doctrine.* Amherst, MA: HRD Press, 2003.

Carkhuff, R. R. and Berenson, B. G., et al. *Freedom-Building.* Amherst, MA: HRD Press, 2003.

Carkhuff, R. R. and Berenson, B. G., et al. *The Freedom Wars.* Amherst, MA: HRD Press, 2005.

Carkhuff, R. R. and Berenson, B. G., et al. *The Possibilities Economy.* Amherst, MA: HRD Press, 2006.

Drasgow, J. Eclipsing All Great Works. Foreword, *The Freedom Wars.* Amherst, MA: HRD Press, 2000.

Einstein, A. *Relativity: The Special and General Theory.* New York: Henry Holt, 1931.

Einstein, A. *The Evolution of Physics.* Cambridge: University of Cambridge, 1938.

Einstein, A. *Collected Papers of Albert Einstein.* Princeton, NJ: Princeton University Press, 1989.

Hebb, D. O. *The Organization of Behavior.* New York: John Wiley and Sons, 1949.

Hull, C. L. *Mathematics—Deductive Theory of Rote Learning.* New York: Appleton–Century–Crofts, 1940.

Hull, C. L. *Principles of Behavior.* New York: Appleton–Century–Crofts, 1943.

Hull, C. L. *A Behavior System.* New Haven, CT: Yale University Press, 1952.

Kakovitch, T. *The Fifth Force.* Amherst, MA: HRD Press, 2012.

Kakovitch, T. *Collegium.* Amherst, MA: HRD Press, 2012.

Kakovitch, T. *Anthropogenics.* Amherst, MA: HRD Press, 2013.

Kakovitch, T. and O'Hara, S. *Physics and the New Economy.* Amherst, MA: HRD Press, 2014.

Kerner, O., et al. National Advisory Commission. *Report on Civil Disorders.* NY: Bantam Books, 1968.

Kilby, J. *First Successful Demonstration of Integrating a Transition with Resistors and Capacitors on a Simple Semiconductor Chip Defining the Monolithic Idea.* Dallas, TX: Texas Instruments, September 12, 1958.

Pavlov, I. P. *Conditioned Reflexes.* Oxford: Oxford University Press, 1927.

Rogers, C. R. The Necessary and Sufficient Conditions of Therapeutic Personality Change. *Journal of Consulting Psychology,* 1957, 22, 95–103.

Siegel, S. *Nonparametric Statistics for the Behavioral Sciences.* Washington, DC: American Association for the Advancement of Science, 1959.

Sprinthall, R. C. *Basic Statistical Analysis.* Boston, MA: Allyn and Bacon, 2011.

Sprinthall, R. C. Psychenomics. Afterword in R. R. Carkhuff, *Saving America: The Generativity Solution.* Amherst, MA: HRD Press, 2010.

Sprinthall, R. C. *SPSS.* Boston, MA: Pearson Education, Inc., 2009.

Straus, E. *Phenomenology: Pure and Applied.* Pittsburgh: Duquesne University Press, 1964.

Truax, C. B. and Carkhuff, R. R. *Toward Effective Counseling and Therapy.* Chicago, IL: Aldine, 1967.

Watson, J. *Behaviorism.* Chicago, IL: University of Chicago Press, 1930.

Information Sciences

Avery, J. *Information Theory and Evolution.* Singapore: World Scientific, 2003.

Bairstow, J. *The Father of the Information Age.* New York: Laser Focus World, 2002.

Bateson, G. *Form, Substance, and Difference in Steps to an Ecology of the Mind.* Chicago, IL: University of Chicago, 1972.

Bekenstein, J. D. Information in the Holographic Universe. *Scientific American,* 2003.

Beynon-Davies, P. *Information Systems: An Introduction to Informatics in Organization.* London: Palgrave, 2002.

Beynon-Davies, P. *Business Information Systems* London: Palgrave, 2009.

Brown, J. S. and Duguid, P. *The Social Life of Information.* Boston, MA: Harvard Business School, 2002.

Casagrande, D. Information as Verb: Re-conceptualizing Information for Cognitive and Ecological Models. *Journal of Ecological Anthropology, 3,* 4–13, 1999.

Dusenbery, D. B. *Sensory Ecology.* New York: Q. R. Freeman, 1992.

Floridi, L. *Information: A Very Short Introduction.* Oxford: Oxford University Press, 2010.

Gleick, J. *What Just Happened: A Chronicle from the Information Frontier.* New York: Pantheon, 2002.

Gleick, J. *The Information: A History, a Theory, a Flood.* New York: Pantheon, 2011.

Goonatilake, S. *The Evolution of Information.* London: Pinter, 1991.

Headrick, D. R. *When Information Came of Age.* Oxford: Oxford University Press, 2000.

Hoagland, M. and Dodson, B. *The Way Life Works.* New York: Random House, 1995.

Liu, A. *The Laws of Cool: Knowledge, Work and the Culture of Information.* Chicago, IL: University of Chicago, 2004.

Pérez-Montoro, M. *The Phenomenon of Information.* Lanham, MD: Scarecrow, 2007.

Roederer, J. G. *Information and Its Role in Nature.* Berlin: Springor, 2005.

Seife, C. *Decoding the Universe.* New York: Viking, 2006.

Solymar, L. *Getting the Message: A History of Communication.* Oxford: Oxford University Press, 1999.

Stewart, T. *Wealth of Knowledge.* New York: Doubleday, 2001.

Vigo, R. Representational Information. *Information Sciences, 181,* 4847–4859, 2011.

Virilio, P. *The Information Bomb.* London: Verso, 2000.

Watson, J. *Behaviorism.* Chicago, IL: University of Chicago Press, 1930.

Wicker, S. B. and Kim, S. *Fundamentals of Codes, Graphs, and Iterative Decoding.* New York: Sprager, 2003.

Yockey, H. P. *Information Theory and the Origins of Life.* Cambridge: Cambridge University Press, 2005.

Young, P. *The Nature of Information.* Westport, CT: Greenwood, 1987.

Carkhuff Body of Work

Robert R. Carkhuff, Ph.D.

The Generativity Solution:
Science in the Service of Humankind

An Annotated Body of Work

CONTENTS

1. Introduction and Overview
2. Helping and Human Relations
3. Educational and Community Applications
4. Human and Organizational Processing
5. Probabilities and Possibilities Sciences
6. New Capitalism and Freedom-Building
7. Generativity and the Human Sciences
8. Summary and Transition

1. Introduction and Overview

Carkhuff was 15 years out of graduate studies in psychology when the world of science first took note of his scientific contributions in the study of helping and human relations.

Today, Carkhuff is the most powerful force in the history of science representing the science and technology of **human generativity** and formulating "the human sciences".

With a profound commitment to establishing a **true science of human behavior,** Carkhuff has been the path-finding leader for the past 50 years as his body of work will testify.

In 1978, in terms of frequency of citations in psychology, Carkhuff ranked among the leading contributors (see Table 3). Two volumes of *Helping and Human Relations* and one volume on *Counseling and Psychotherapy* led the listings.

Table 3.
Most-Cited Books in Clinical Psychology [1]

Bandura, A. *Principles of Behavior Modification,* 1969.

Carkhuff, R. R. *Helping and Human Relations, Volumes I and II,* 1969.

Kelly, G. A. *The Psychology of Personal Constructs,* 1955.

Truax, C. B. and Carkhuff, R. R. *Toward Effective Counseling and Psychotherapy,* 1967.

Fenichel, O. *The Psychoanalytic Theory of Neurosis,* 1945

Freud, S. *Zur Geschichte der Psychoanalytischen Bewegung (On the History of the Psychoanalytic Movement),* 1914.

2. Helping and Human Relations

Carkhuff led the revolution of the helping professions from theoretical to operational treatment in the late 1960s. He and his associates defined the effective ingredients of helping in operational terms:

- *Toward Effective Counseling and Psychotherapy.* Chicago, IL: Aldine, 1967 (with C. B. Truax).

- *Sources of Gain in Counseling and Psychotherapy.* New York: Holt, Rinehart & Winston, 1967 (with B. G. Berenson).

- *Beyond Counseling and Therapy.* New York: Holt, Rinehart & Winston, 1967.

Basically, the helping dimensions, such as empathy and respect, facilitated helpee exploration leading to indices of therapeutic personality change. The book with Truax (Aldine, 1967) was listed among the most-cited books in clinical psychology. [2]

Carkhuff extended these core findings to all helping and human relations. Simultaneously, he developed training programs for learning these operational skills in the practice of helping:

- *Helping and Human Relations. Volume I: Selection and Training.* New York: Holt, Rinehart & Winston, 1969

- *Helping and Human Relations. Volume II: Practice and Research.* New York: Holt, Rinehart & Winston, 1969

- *The Art of Helping.* Amherst, MA: HRD Press, 1971

Operationally, the helper's skills were refined to emphasize responding, personalizing, and initiating in order to facilitate the helpee's process, which was expanded to incorporate exploring, understanding, and acting, all of which led to therapeutic change. Now in its ninth edition, *The Art of Helping* has sold more than one million copies. In turn, the two volumes of *Helping and Human Relations* were among the most-cited books in social sciences. [3]

Along with his three books, Carkhuff was, himself, identified among the most-referenced social scientists by *The Institute of Scientific Information.* [4] [5] [6] Altogether, these works culminated the operationalization of previously theoretical processes.

3. Educational and Community Applications

In the 1970s and 1980s, Carkhuff transferred his findings to human and community development in the private as well as public sectors:

- *The Development of Human Resources: Education, Society and Social Action.* New York: Holt, Rinehart & Winston, 1971

- *Toward Actualizing Human Potential.* Amherst, MA: HRD Press, 1981

- *The Exemplar: The Exemplary Performer in the Age of Productivity.* Amherst, MA: HRD Press, 1983

- *Sources of Human Productivity.* Amherst, MA: HRD Press, 1984

Operationally, Carkhuff defined the productive human performer in the productive organizational system that, in turn, is defined in the productive community development system.

John T. Kelly, Director Emeritus, Advanced Systems Design, IBM, Inc., offered this evaluation of Carkhuff's work:

> **Carkhuff offers us a vision of the future. It is a vision of a great Age of Productivity, an age in which the human products and services are effectively increased so that all people can share. It is a vision of an age in which the resource inputs, natural and otherwise, are effectively invested so that no people are deprived of their birthrights.**
>
> (Kelly, Foreword, *Sources of Human Productivity,*
> 1984, p. xii)

During this period, Carkhuff and his associates launched a series of training products in teaching, training, and instructional systems design:

- *The Skills of Teaching Series, Volumes I–VI.* Amherst, MA: HRD Press, 1977–1981

- *Instructional Systems Design, Volumes I and II.* Amherst, MA: HRD Press, 1984

- *Training Delivery Skills, Volumes I and II.* Amherst, MA: HRD Press, 1984

Systematically, these works broke teaching and training down into four skill sets: interpersonal skills, content development skills, lesson planning skills, teaching delivery and classroom management skills. The educational initiatives culminated in the issue of the journal, *Education,* dedicated to Carkhuff. [7]

4. Human and Organizational Processing

In the late 1980s, Carkhuff created systematic skills for human processing or thinking with applications for the development of **Human and Information Capital:**

- *Interpersonal Skills and Human Productivity.* Amherst, MA: HRD Press, 1984

- *Human Processing and Human Productivity.* Amherst, MA: HRD Press, 1986

- *The Age of the New Capitalism.* Amherst, MA: HRD Press, 1988

- *Empowering: The Creative Leader in the Age of the New Capitalism.* Amherst, MA: HRD Press, 1989

Carkhuff's mentor, B. R. Bugelski, a protégé of Clark Hull, one of the founders of American psychology, commented as follows:

> **This work rationalizes all of our efforts in learning theory and promises the culmination of psychology in a science of processing.**
>
> (Bugelski, Review, *Human Processing and Human Productivity,* 1984)

Carkhuff summarizes the research of the effects of individual, interpersonal, and organizational processing systems in hundreds of studies of more than 150,000 recipients. Basically, Carkhuff defined Human Capital Development or HCD as generative thinking. Carkhuff's work was reviewed by the distinguished social scientist, C. H. Patterson, University of Illinois:

> **This revolution has an important social significance also. I have stated elsewhere that the extent to which a society and its institutions, including its economic systems, facilitate the development of self-actualizing persons constitutes the criterion for the goodness of that society. To the extent that our society incorporates Carkhuff's system, it will become a better society for all its members.**
>
> (Patterson, Foreword, *Interpersonal Skills and Human Productivity,* 1983, p. 5)

5. Probabilities and Possibilities Sciences

In the 1990s and 2000s, Carkhuff, Berenson, and associates introduced the "Science of Possibilities" to drive the historical "Science of Probabilities":

- *The New Science of Possibilities, Volume I. The Processing Science.* Amherst, MA: HRD Press, 2000

- *The New Science of Possibilities, Volume II. The Processing Technologies.* Amherst, MA: HRD Press, 2000

- *Human Possibilities.* Amherst, MA: HRD Press, 2000

- *The Possibilities Leader.* Amherst, MA: HRD Press, 2000

- *The Possibilities Organization.* Amherst, MA: HRD Press, 2000

- *The Possibilities Economy.* Amherst, MA: HRD Press, 2005

Dr. David N. Aspy, renowned scientist, educator, and protégé of Robert Oppenheimer, commented on Carkhuff's contribution to the advancement of civilization:

> **To support his views, Carkhuff does not simply offer up the science of science. He also presents the most exhaustive body of research and demonstration on relating and empowering ever presented in behavioral science. Moreover, he engaged in the most advanced demonstrations of phenomenal potential, including human, ever attempted...**
>
> **Together, these process-centric breakthroughs will lead us to a grand new Age of Enlightenment—The Age of Ideation, and in the process, The Science of Freedom.**
>
> (Aspy, *Window on the Universe, The Science of Freedom* 2007, p. 224)

6. New Capitalism and Freedom-Building

Eighteen months after having been introduced to Carkhuff's book, *"The Age of the New Capitalism,"* (1988), Pope John Paul II issued his Papal Encyclical, **"The New Capitalism."** In it, the Pope conceded the prepotent power of **human generativity** and committed himself to the **free economy** as the only alternative after the failure of Communism:

Can it perhaps be said that, after the failure of Communism, capitalism is the victorious social system, and that capitalism should be the goal of countries now making efforts to rebuild their economy and society?

If by "capitalism" is meant an economic system that recognizes the fundamental and positive role of business, the market, private property, and the resulting responsibility for the measure of production, as well as free human creativity in the economic sector, then the answer is certainly in the affirmative, even though it would perhaps be more appropriate to speak of a "business economy," "market economy," or simply "free economy." (John Paul II, **Centesimus Annus**, 42.1–42.2, in Miller, *Encyclicals*)

Source: Carkhuff, R. R. *The Freedom Wars.* HRD Press, 2004

Early in the 21st century, Carkhuff and associates introduced the models and systems for freedom-building:

- *The Freedom Doctrine.* Amherst, MA: HRD Press, 2003
- *Freedom-Building.* Amherst, MA: HRD Press, 2004
- *The Freedom Wars.* Amherst, MA: HRD Press, 2004

In evaluating the contributions of Carkhuff to the advancement of civilization, John R. Cannon, Chief Executive Officer, Human Technology, Inc., summarizes Carkhuff's contributions [8] [9]:

> **Together, these works represent the contributions of The Possibilities Science to generating The Human and Ideational Sciences that define The Science of Freedom.**
>
> **In this context, there is nothing more powerful than the human brain enriched by possibilities experience… All of his books and all of his demonstrations, collectively from the earliest to the latest, are the products of this processing phenomenon, profound alternatives for individuals, organizations, communities, cultures, and nations; indeed, for The Global Village and its Marketplace. The Sources of Freedom are Possibilities!**
>
> (Cannon, Preface, *Science of Freedom,* 2007, p. xiii)

7. Generativity and the Human Sciences

Carkhuff's lifelong passion has been generativity or generative human processing. His recent work has focused on resolving the socioeconomic problems of our time through generative processing at all levels of community, culture, and economy:

- *The Generativity Solution, Building the New Economy.* Amherst, MA: HRD Press, 2009

- *The Generativity Solution, Volume III: Community Generativity.* Amherst, MA: HRD Press, 2009

- *The Generativity Solution, Volume IV: Cultural Generativity.* Amherst, MA: HRD Press, 2009

- *The Generativity Solution, Volume V: Economic Generativity.* Amherst, MA: HRD Press, 2009

Working with his colleagues, his body of work has culminated in a series introducing the **Human Sciences:**

- *Human Generativity: An Introduction to the Human Sciences.* Amherst, MA: HRD Press, 2013

- *The Human Sciences, Volume I: Probabilities, Possibilities, and Generativity Sciences.* Amherst, MA: HRD Press, 2013

- *The Human Sciences, Volume II: Probabilities, Possibilities, and Generativity Technologies.* Amherst, MA: HRD Press, 2013

- *The Human Sciences, Volume III: Carkhuff and Human Generativity.* Amherst, MA: HRD Press, 2013 (by B. G. Berenson)

Barry Cohen, Executive Vice President, Parametric Technology Corporation, summarizes Carkhuff's contributions as follows:

> **His body of research has constituted the foundation for revolutions in all areas of human endeavor: human, information, and organizational resource development: government, corporate and community development; cultural, national, and now global economic growth. In short, he has changed the world by making social science a "true science."**

> (Cohen, Foreword, *Generativity Solution,* 2009, p. ix)

Hernan Oyarzabal, Executive Director Emeritus, International Monetary Fund, summarizes Carkhuff's theory of the prepotency of generativity as follows:

> **It is indeed the "Generativity of Human Brainpower" and not the "Economic Theory of Stasis" that hold the interdependent, enlightened, and entrepreneurial keys to our Prosperous, Participatory, and Peaceful future.**

> (Oyarzabal, An Open Letter on the Economy,
> *Generativity Solution,* 2009, p. xiii)

8. Summary and Transition

In summary, Carkhuff's body of work has differentiated him from all others in the history of science. Primary among his contributions has been the operationalization and application of **possibilities science and generativity.**

Carkhuff's greatest contributions may lie ahead—the transfers of possibilities science to his current list of generativity projects in a troubled world. It is left to his lifelong colleague, Bernard G. Berenson, an Einsteinian scholar, to place Carkhuff's work in historical perspective:

> **Carkhuff's contributions to universal processing, alone, qualify him for leadership among the greatest scientists of history. His "nesting, encoding, and rotating of processing systems" are the core processes of Nature's Generativity. In creating The Human Sciences, Carkhuff belongs in the Pantheon of Science along with the works of DaVinci, Newton, and Einstein.**
>
> (Berenson, B. G. We Can Be Beams of Light.
> Foreword, *Human Sciences, Volume II*
> Amherst, MA: HRD Press, 2013)

In this context, Carkhuff is dedicated to the values of Albert Einstein, his exemplar:

> **It is a very high goal: free and responsible development of the individual, so that he may place his powers freely and gladly in the service of all mankind.**
>
> (Einstein, *An Ideal of Service to Our Fellow Man*,
> 1950, p. 59)

Where Carkhuff joined the list of established contributors to Psychology in 1978, he now stands alone as the dominant force defining the **Human, Information, and Organizational Sciences** in the 21st century science and technology.

Along with his associates, he has architected and implemented new platforms for the following:

- **Generative Human Sciences**
- **Human-Centric Information Sciences**
- **Human-Centric Organizational Sciences**
- **Human-Centric Economic Sciences**
- **Generative Civilizations**

In so doing, Carkhuff and his associates have outperformed the entire body of the social sciences and provided leadership for the declining body of the physical sciences.

His colleague, Dr. Tom Kakovitch, a physical scientist, has the final word on generativity:

> **Nature grows with generativity. That is why no one holds a monopoly over intelligence.**
>
> (Kakovitch, *Collegium*, 2012)

[1]   Garfield, E. *The 100 Books Most Cited by Social Scientists.* Number 37, Institute for Scientific Information.

[2]   Garfield, E. *The 100 Books Most Cited by Social Scientists.* Number 37, Institute for Scientific Information.

[3]   Garfield, E. *The 100 Books Most Cited by Social Scientists.* Number 37, Institute for Scientific Information.

[4]   Garfield, E. *The 100 Books Most Cited by Social Scientists.* Number 45, Institute for Scientific Information.

[5]   Endler, Rushtore, and Rogdeger. Productivity and Scholarly Impact. *American Psychologist,* Vol. 33, No. 12, 1062–1082.

[6]   Heesacker, Heppner, and Rogers. Classics and Emerging Classics. *Journal of Counseling Psychology,* Vol. 29, No. 4, 400–406.

[7]   Carkhuff, R. R. Leader in Human Resource Development. *Education,* Vol. 106, No. 3.

[8]   Berenson, B. G. and Cannon, J. R. *The Science of Freedom.* McLean, VA: American Noble Prize, 2007.

[9]   Carkhuff, R. R. *The Age of Ideation.* McLean, VA: American Noble Prize, 2007.

www.carkhuff.com

www.mcleanproject.com

www.carkhuffgenerativitylibrary.com

www.ingramcontent.com/pod-product-compliance
Lightning Source LLC
Chambersburg PA
CBHW081506200326
41518CB00015B/2404